Seed Thoughts For Loving Yourself

CULTIVATING
the garden of your mind

DAY BY DAY

Suzanne E. Harrill, M.Ed.

Seed Thoughts For Loving Yourself
Cultivating the Garden of Your Mind
Day by Day

© Suzanne E. Harrill 2007

First published by Innerworks Publishing

ISBN 9-781-883648-16-9

Innerworks Publishing
167 Glengarry Place
Castle Rock, CO 80108

www.InnerworksPublishing.com

This is a revised edition of
Affirm Your Self Day by Day:
Seed Thoughts for Loving Your Self
Softcover 1991 ISBN 0-9625996-1-1
Hardcover 1998 ISBN1-883648-22-X

This book is dedicated to my parents:

John and Mary Shaw

Special Thanks to:

Diane Langley
Marle Creer
Peggy Floyd
Loretta Lewis
Danna Malcolm
Nancy Moonstarr

Cover and book design by Val Price
valgalprice@hotmail.com
303.319.8348

Foreword by John Randolph Price

"Every day is a new beginning." We smile at such a cliché, not realizing the profound significance of the pure truth it contains, for through the darkness of night the old passes away and the light of dawn signifies a new day and a new life — if we capitalize on the opportunity.

An ancient teaching says that the beginning thought upon awakening sets the tone for the rest of the day. Considering this, I was reminded of once watching and listening to a quartet preparing to sing. The leader hummed a note and the others caught it and enthusiastically plunged into song on the same key, at the right pitch. They took advantage of a new beginning and issued forth a chorus of success — because they were in tune with the universal principle of harmony.

That's what this book is all about — getting a jump-start each morning with the proper tone and pitch and continuing in the right rhythm throughout the rest of the day. Ralph Waldo Emerson wrote, "We are what we think about all day long… the good mind is known by the choice of what is positive, of what is advancing. We must embrace the affirmative." What do most of us think about all day long? Usually it's what we do not want rather than what we do, and the primary reason for this is a sense of unworthiness. We have forgotten who we are — the highest of creation and the completeness of the universe —

heirs to all that is good, true, and beautiful. But with forgetting also comes remembering — a change of mind — and we have the power to choose that which is positive, to choose what is advancing. Day by day we can etch deeply into our personal consciousness the truth of our being and transform our self-image and self-esteem, becoming new creatures on the side of life where wonders never cease.

The word *consciousness* is an enigma to many people, yet it's nothing more than the awareness, understanding, and knowledge of our identity. And as this self-image expands to encompass our Spiritual Self, the attributes of that Self begin to be reflected in the phenomenal world and miracles become the order of the day.

Suzanne is one of those practical writers who blends intellectual expertise and spiritual understanding with meaningful personal experiences. The result is a model for consciousness expansion — to help us realize our power through a deeper awareness, understanding, and knowledge of who and what we truly are.

In *Seed Thoughts For Loving Yourself* she takes us on a full year's course of New Beginnings — using delightful seed thoughts to plant in the garden of our minds to change our beliefs, thus changing our lives. Assume the role of the gardener and follow Suzanne's recommended sowing sequence.

Let your mind be cultivated daily and water the seeds with fertile expectations, while also making sure that the weeds of trouble and discontent are continually uprooted. Do your part with dedication and enthusiasm, and a rich and bountiful harvest will be yours.

John Randolph Price is an internationally known lecturer and bestselling author of eighteen nonfiction books: *The Angels Within Us, Angel Energy, Living a Life of Joy, The Superbeings, The Abundance Book, The Alchemist's Handbook, Empowerment, The Jesus Code, The Love Book, The Meditation Book, Practical Spirituality, A Spiritual Philosophy for the New World, The Success Book, The Wellness Book, With Wings As Eagles, The Workbook for Self-Mastery* (formerly titled *The Planetary Commission*), *Removing the Masks That Bind Us,* and *Nothing Is Too Good To Be True.*

Visit his web site: www.johnrandolphprice.com.

John and his wife, Jan Price, started the Quartus Foundation in 1981 and are the founders of World Healing Day, which originated on December 31, 1986. Visit their web site: www.quartus.org.

*The Acorn Analogy

Deep inside you know how to be you,
  as an acorn knows how to be a mighty oak.

The acorn does the best it can do
  at each stage of growth along its life path.

Even if the early start was less than perfect
  the eager oak accelerates its desire to grow
  every time it receives nurturing from nature:
  sunlight, rainwater, and soil nutrients.

YOU are like the acorn doing your best
  under the conditions in which you are growing.

Nurture yourself with awareness, acceptance, love,
  self-respect, and self-esteem, then watch
  yourself grow toward your full-potential Self!

* *This analogy summarizes the teachings
  of this book.*

Introduction

May this daily affirmation book inspire you to plant new ideas, concepts, and thoughts in the garden of your mind or remind you of truths that you already know. Your mind is like the receptive soil in a garden. Many of the thoughts and beliefs growing there are not giving you the results you desire, so need to be weeded. You are like a gardener cultivating and caring for the thoughts and beliefs that grow in the garden of your mind. Each day of reading seed thoughts is an opportunity to repattern your thinking and update your belief system to new levels of truth. When you change negative, self-critical, fearful thoughts into positive, accepting, problem-solving, loving ones, you experience a shift in how you feel.

As you change how you feel on the inside, you will find a desire growing to make positive behavioral changes. Your inner dialog with yourself will transform, too. These seed thoughts have the power to influence and improve your self-talk, which is a major way to create better results in your life. Consequently, these changes allow you to experience your life in ways that attract acceptance, forgiveness, and solutions to problems. Whether you are new to the journey of self-discovery or a seasoned traveler, use this daily guide to help build and maintain a loving relationship with yourself and the world around you.

A major theme in this book is how to feel better about yourself by building your feelings of self-worth. Experiencing sound self-esteem is to grow daily in accepting the beauty and perfection of who you really are, your true Self (soul, essence, higher Self, authentic Self, Christ Self, God Self, Buddha Nature, etc.). Learning to accept that you are a spiritual being allows you to experience unconditional love from higher, more expanded, and aware parts of your being. As you allow this spiritual part of you that is all knowing and exists beyond our world to love you without conditions, you grow in feeling worthy, understanding that your life counts and makes a difference. You discover the importance of healing the negativity from your past by working through unprocessed feelings. Forgiving yourself and others for unwise behaviors, beliefs, attitudes, decisions, and habits releases old interpretations and feelings about being a victim of others and of life experiences. Instead of restricting yourself to your past, you are free in the present moment to take full responsibility for your own life and to know you can create a better future for yourself.

Daily, as you grow in your ability to feel warm and loving toward yourself, you will automatically pass unconditional love, tolerance, understanding, acceptance, forgiveness, and awareness on to other people; people treat others the way they treat themselves. Feeling good within allows you to naturally convey good things to others. Forgiveness of others, by the way, does not mean you agree with or support their negative words or actions. It means you have learned what you could from the situations, grieved your losses, and are ready to remove yourself from perpetuating the drama. No longer are you at the effect of their negativity. You can move on with your life.

Before the daily affirmations begin on January 1 there are two important methods to help you get started loving yourself: a self-esteem inventory and The Twelve Steps for Building Self-Esteem. Begin by taking the Self-Esteem Awareness Inventory (after the introduction), then take it again after a year of reading this book to watch your progress. It does not tell you your level of self-esteem; it simply shows you areas where your belief system influences your self-esteem and where you might need to change some of your thinking patterns. Again, as you update the beliefs guiding your life to higher truths you will improve how you feel about yourself. Following the inventory is a definition of self-esteem and characteristics of high self-esteem to help you see the direction in which you are growing.

A sound spiritual path encouraging self-inquiry and personal transformation is the Twelve Steps of Alcoholics Anonymous. I have rewritten The Twelve Steps for healing low self-esteem; they are included in this book. Those of you already using the original Twelve Steps may want to continue with that program.

Affirmations are positive statements that, when repeated over and over, help to repattern dysfunctional thoughts and beliefs that are already in place in your mind. Each sentence in the daily passages can stand alone as an affirmation, and the last sentence on the page, the daily affirmation, is one you can use throughout the day. Repeat this daily affirmation to yourself several times throughout the day. You might, for example, say it every time you walk through a doorway, look at your watch, or when you feel challenged, uncomfortable, upset, or angry. It also helps to plant the ideas more powerfully in your mind when you write down each affirmation ten times a day. Read the passage for the day when you wake up and when you go to bed, out loud when possible.

There was a time in my life when many of the ideas in this book were new to me. Not only did I not have the belief system to hold them, I thought many of them were false. One idea in particular stands out in my mind where I had no clue what the higher truth was. A teacher said to me in one of our discussions, "No one can make you angry without your agreement." I just walked away thinking to myself, "What a crazy idea, of course other people make me angry." Then, I went through all the things going wrong with my life and the people who caused them, thus perpetuating my victim consciousness.

It took many years and a lot of pondering, reading self-help books, taking self-discovery workshops, talking with wise people, counseling, meditating, journal writing, and inner work to comprehend ideas like the one my teacher had presented. Today, it is an automatic part of my belief system that other people do NOT make me angry and I know without a doubt that I have to have something matching the situation to even *feel* angry. I alone am responsible for my reactions and feelings to people and situations. Now, I go within and look at myself when "someone makes me angry," to figure out what I had to do with the situation and what I want to do to change it. This empowers me to not be a victim of what others say or do and to live my life with more peace and harmony.

The same may be true for you when reading this book. When an idea startles you or makes you react, simply pause and consider this might be one of the concepts to delve a little deeper into before being able to accept it. Take your time. It took a long time to gather all the ideas growing in the garden of your mind. It is hard to tell which ones are the weeds sometimes. As the gardener of your mind, slowly look at the thoughts and beliefs that need to be pulled. Use the seed thoughts in this book for consideration to help you plant new ones. I share only what I have proven to be true for myself from my intense study and exploration of Truth on my personal journey. If an affirmation is too much of a stretch for you and your negative self-talk goes haywire telling you it is impossible, then consider changing the first couple of words. For example, change "I am worthy" to "I am learning that I am worthy," or "I am considering I am worthy."

I encourage you to extend love to others by placing the name of a loved one, a friend, or a special person on the page corresponding to the day of their birth. You will then be able to include them in your prayers, meditations, and focus for that day. The love growing within you then radiates secretly to all those within your world. If you are uncomfortable with certain spiritual words, such as *God* or *higher*

Self, please substitute the word that is your personal preference, such as *Higher Power*, *Universe*, *Universal Mind*, *Source*, *Creator*, *Christ*, *Energy*, *Life*, *Spirit*, or *All That Is*. It is my intention to reach people of all faiths, as well as those who are triggered by certain religious words. Universal Truth that speaks to you is what is important. May this book help you stop negative thinking patterns that keep you stuck in low self-esteem, and nourish you to remember your innate worth.

*Namaste,

Suzanne

* *I honor the place in you of wholeness, love, light, truth, and beauty. When you are in that place in you and I am in that place in me, there is only one of us.*

Self-Esteem Awareness Inventory

Rate yourself on each with a scale of 0 to 4 based upon your current thoughts, feelings, and behaviors: 0 = I never think, feel, or behave this way. 1 = I do less than half the time. 2 = I do 50% of the time. 3 = I do more than half the time. 4 = I always think, feel, or behave this way.

Score	Self-Esteem Statements
_____	1. I like and accept myself as I am right now, today, even as I grow and evolve.
_____	2. I am worthy simply for who I am, not what I do. I do not have to earn my worthiness.
_____	3. I get my needs met before meeting the wants of others. I balance my needs with those of my partner and family.
_____	4. I easily release negative feelings from other's judgments and focus instead on living my life with integrity and to the best of my abilities.
_____	5. I always tell myself the truth about what I am feeling.

_____ 6. I am incomparable and stop comparing myself with other people.

_____ 7. I feel of equal value to other people, regardless of my performance, looks, IQ, achievements, or possessions.

_____ 8. I am my own authority. I make decisions with the intention of furthering my own and others' best interests.

_____ 9. I learn and grow from my mistakes rather than deny them or use them to confirm my unworthiness.

_____ 10. I stop my critical self-talk and replace it with a nurturing, kind, encouraging voice.

_____ 11. I love, respect, and honor myself.

_____ 12. I am not responsible for anyone else's actions, needs, choices, thoughts, moods, or feelings — only for my own.

_____ 13. I do not dominate others or allow others to dominate me.

_____ 14. I have good physical and emotional boundaries with others.

_____ 15. I feel my own feelings and think my own thoughts, even when those around me think or feel differently.

_____ 16. I stop using "shoulds" and "oughts," which are value judgments that put me or another down. (It is irrelevant what I should have done or should do. It is more important to know what I am willing to do and not do.)

_____ 17. I am responsible for changing what I do not like in my life. I face my problems, fears, and insecurities and take appropriate steps to heal and grow.

_____ 18. I am a person of my word and follow through on the things I commit to do.

_____ 19. I forgive myself and others for making mistakes and being unaware.

_____ 20. I believe my life counts. I find meaning and have purpose in my life.

_____ 21. I deserve love and happiness even when others blame or criticize me, for I cannot control what others think about me.

_____ 22. I take care of myself on all levels:
physical, social, emotional, mental,
and spiritual.

_____ 23. I spend quality time with myself on a
regular basis.

_____ 24. I release unreal expectations for
myself and others.

_____ 25. I choose to love and respect all human
beings regardless of their beliefs
and actions, whether or not I have a
personal relationship with them.

This is not a test or a precise measure of self-esteem. It identifies beliefs, feelings, and behaviors that contribute to your self-esteem. The 25 statements can be used to update beliefs that have limited your self-esteem. Use the statements as affirmations to change old, outdated beliefs that keep you stuck in low self-esteem. Repeat the statements to yourself often, emphasizing your low-scoring answers.

What Is Self-Esteem?

Self-esteem is how you feel about yourself based upon your personal evaluation of yourself. Your self-concept, beliefs, and perceptions of yourself all influence your self-esteem and may or may not be accurate. The early experiences of life conditioned your personal evaluation, some positively and some negatively. Early on, the family of origin, teachers, peers, and social institutions such as schools and churches influenced your self-esteem. The good news is that as an adult you now have the power to assess your own self-esteem, at the conscious level of understanding, to determine what needs to be improved upon and changed.

Happiness, self-empowerment, satisfaction in work, good relationships, and success are all built upon a solid foundation of healthy self-esteem. Love, respect, forgiveness, and tolerance for self and all others are valued. Healthy self-esteem is based on an internal frame of reference for loving and accepting self rather than the external (relying on what other people say or do).

High self-esteem is a quiet comfortable feeling of acceptance and love for yourself as you are. It is respecting yourself while honestly seeing your good and not-so-good qualities. High self-esteem is characterized by congruence between inner states (beliefs, feelings, attitudes) and outer states (behaviors, relationships, health).

Remember, most people have room to grow in the process of loving, respecting, and accepting themselves. The first step in healing low self-esteem is to recognize where the problems hide. Most people benefit from changing negative self-talk and updating beliefs.

Signs of High Self-Esteem

- Remembering to honor yourself from within and to detach from the negative comments and opinions of others.

- Spending time with people who accept and support you.

- Learning from mistakes and being able to say, "I made a mistake, I'm sorry."

- Taking responsibility for your own perceptions and reactions and not projecting onto others.

- Ability to listen to your inner self and act on this guidance.

- Growing in self-respect, self-confidence, and self-acceptance.

- Honestly assessing your strengths and weaknesses without excessive pride or shame.

- Recognizing areas of yourself needing improvement and areas needing acceptance.

- Growing in awareness and taking positive risks.

- Balancing activities with quiet, quality, alone time.

- Accepting consequences of your choices, thoughts, feelings, and behaviors.

- Catching negative self-talk and changing it to a positive, supportive voice.

- Desiring to grow and improve.

- Being your own best friend.

About the Twelve Steps

I have rewritten the Twelve Steps of Alcoholics Anonymous for people working on the universal need to love and accept themselves. Many people who read the original Twelve Steps have a problem stating "I am powerless." Those people who practice reprogramming their subconscious minds through positive affirmation do not believe in stating a negative such as this.

I find it helpful to talk about the self in two parts: the little self (ego, conditioned self, or personality self) and the true Self (spiritual Self, transpersonal Self, Christ Self, authentic Self, or higher Self). In reality there is no split; they are one. Until a person experiences this oneness, however, it seems as if there is a separation or split. The Twelve Steps of Building Self-Esteem address this split. By practicing this process of healing through these Twelve Steps, one is capable of experiencing the truth, which is wholeness.

The Twelve Steps move a person from the powerless state of consciousness of the little self to an empowered Spiritually Awakened Being. The personality self is created from the past and is subject to addiction, pain, illusion, and fear. The experiences of childhood conditioned the personality. Since most parenting was not totally adequate (no blame implied), the personality self gets stuck wanting what it never received in the past. This focus on the past of pain, deprivation, etc. creates the split from the true Self. The Twelve Steps help you on the spiritual journey of knowing who you truly are: a Spiritual Being having a physical experience.

Twelve Steps of AA Adapted to Building Self-Esteem

1. I admit my little self (ego, conditioned self) is powerless to control my negative thoughts and feelings. My life of feeling unworthy is not working and is unmanageable.

2. I believe my wholeness depends on experiencing Love from my Higher Power.

3. I choose to turn my life over to the care and direction of my Higher Power to become fully conscious, a self-actualized being.

4. I continue to know myself, looking at past behavior, guiding beliefs, choices, and conditioning from my family of origin that have manifested negatively in my life.

5. I admit and forgive myself for fearful, unaware life-choices, thoughts, words, actions, and reactions that have blocked Love in my life.

6. I am ready to transform all aspects of myself that block the power of Love in my life.

7. I humbly ask my Higher Power to achieve this transformation.

8. I make a list of all the situations and people whom I believe I have hurt or whom I feel have hurt me because of unawareness. I am willing to make peace with and forgive my past.

9. I heal these relationships directly when possible.

10. I continue to expand my awareness and heal negative patterns that I see. I admit my mistakes and faulty thinking openly and take responsibility for my life.

11. I experience more and more Love consciously from my Higher Power through prayer, meditation, and contemplation. I choose to consciously express this Divine Love through me.

12. I am an awakening spiritual being as a result of practicing these steps. I continue to practice these principles in order to love myself and to pass it on to all others. I generously share this love and awareness with others who choose my assistance.

New Beginning

It's a brand new year and I have a new
beginning, a fresh new start.

I let go of yesterday's resistance to creating a
healthier and happier life.

I begin with a choice to love and
support myself.

I release old negative patterns so I can fully
live this day and all others.

I spend quiet time to ponder the good things
I want to explore this year.

I commit to discovering and being
exactly who I am.

***I set new patterns in motion,
enjoying a new beginning.***

Potential

I spend quiet time walking outside or journal writing to explore my potential.

I imagine the most wonderful future for myself and think about small steps I must take to actualize this future.

I see myself striving and reaching forward, meeting and expressing my potential.

I am like the acorn, full of potential, ready to sprout and begin growing into a giant oak tree.

As it's never too late for the mighty oak to grow new branches, it's never too late for me to grow things such as confidence, self-acceptance, and expressing my true nature.

---

*I am growing daily as my
potential unfolds.*

Worthiness

I am a unique expression of the Source.

I am a worthwhile human being because
I have been created and I am alive.

I am worthy and have value regardless
of whether I have accepted this or not.

I cannot earn being worthy of love, happiness,
and acceptance; it is my birthright.

I sow new seeds in my garden to accept
the truth that I am of value and
an important part of life.

*I am worthy and feel
my life has value.*

Self-Appreciation

I appreciate myself now, just the way I am.

I understand that there are things I want to
change about myself, and know I will.

I stop being overly critical and expecting
too much from myself.

I go at my own pace to change and grow.

As I love and appreciate myself today,
it helps me feel deserving of what
I want to create in my future.

***I appreciate and accept
myself right now, today.***

Unconditional Love

I love and accept myself unconditionally.

At times when I feel lonely, unhappy, or in need of love and acceptance, I turn inward to receive this love from my spiritual Self.

I no longer rely on others for my warm and loving feelings, as others may have their own issues and needs and not be able to respond as I wish.

I do accept and enjoy unconditional love and acceptance from others.

As unconditional love grows within me, the more I'm able to love others.

*I love myself
unconditionally.*

Nurturing

I look for ways to nurture myself.

I visualize possible ways to take
better care of myself.

I write in my journal about people and
experiences that nurture me.

I take time to listen and respond to my inner
needs, such as spending quality time
with myself.

I receive nurturing from simple pleasures, such
as sharing a good meal with a friend, enjoying
the cloud patterns in the sky, the fragrance of a
flower, the colors in a painting, or being with
a favorite pet.

I like sitting or walking in nature where I quiet
my mind and feel my oneness with all of life.

---

*I do one thing today
that nurtures me.*

Responsibility

I take responsibility for my life.

Only I have the power to create my
life the way I want it.

I realize people and events have influenced and
conditioned me, yet I do not blame or hold
others responsible for who I am today.

I choose to grow and work on my awareness,
searching to understand what motivates me to
think, feel, and act as I do.

I see myself taking the risks necessary to
improve my life and to express my true nature.

*I am responsible
for my own life.*

Choices

I am my own authority and make my
own choices.

Not making a choice, I realize, is a choice, too.

I no longer turn my power over to others to
make decisions for me, because I see that I pay
the consequences of their choices.

I willingly pay the consequences, both good and
bad, for my own choices.

By making my own choices and taking
responsibility for them, I expand my free-will
choice and feel I have control over my life.

*I am my own authority and
enjoy making aware choices.*

Feeling Good

I go within myself to feel good.

It feels good to discover who I am and to express my true Self.

Feeling good about myself is no longer dependent upon my achievements, what others think of me, my physical traits, etc.

I feel good about striving to be a better person, doing my best, setting goals, taking risks to meet these goals, and living with deeper meaning and purpose.

It feels good to creatively express my inner truth and beauty.

*I feel good as I allow my
inner spirit to shine.*

Inner Knowing

I listen to the wisdom of my inner knowing.

I take a few moments, right now, to close my eyes, breathe deeply, and go inward.

I go to my place of peace and ask, "What do I need today to feel more balanced? Do I need more activity or less? Do I need to focus on my social, physical, or emotional well-being? What is the next step for expanding my awareness?"

Only I know the answers to these questions.

*I listen to the quiet voice
of my inner knowing.*

Achieving

I enjoy achieving my personal goals and reaching my standards of excellence.

I let go of seeking approval and value from others through my achievements.

I now do things because I enjoy expressing the creative power within me.

I accept the rhythm of cycles with high levels of accomplishment as well as low levels of accomplishment.

I know I am equally worthy whether I get a lot done or I am simply "being" and not accomplishing measurable things.

During the quiet, inward cycles, the seeds of new goals and future achievements are sprouting and taking root.

I enjoy my creative power to express and achieve what pleases me.

Comparison

I stop comparing myself with others,
only with myself to gauge my progress.

I no longer aggressively race to win or to
be the best in the eyes of the world.

I am a winner whether someone is ahead
of me or behind me on the journey of life.

No one is better than or less than I am.

I no longer need to concern myself with
how much progress I'm making by
looking at others, only myself.

I have a special assignment that only I can
fulfill and that is to be "Me."

I accept my own internal time schedule in
allowing my true Self to unfold.

---

*I am incomparable, so I stop
comparing myself to others.*

Awareness

I seek greater awareness.

I want to consciously know the many things that are hidden from my view.

I want to understand everything that has molded my character, both positive and negative, so I can heal and choose wisely how to go forward.

I am empowered by understanding my life and what motivates me.

I expand my awareness by reading, observing myself and others, and thinking about why I do things.

I allow people wiser than myself to guide me.

I welcome my growth in awareness.

Free-Will Choice

I have the power of choice to make
decisions that support my growth.

I let go of what others want for me and make
my choices by listening to my inner Self, paying
attention to my real needs, values, and goals.

I have greater free-will choice
when I know myself.

Today, I support myself by making
choices from my inner place of power.

*I have greater free-will choice
because I listen to myself.*

Past Suffering

Today, I release suffering over painful events experienced in my past.

I stop allowing a difficult childhood or marriage, a physical challenge, or any negative-feeling experiences to cripple this present day.

I see with detachment and clarity what took place in my past; I forgive and then let it go.

I allow hidden emotions to surface so that I can work through them and grieve.

In order not to repeat patterns, I remember my truth about what happened and let it be real.

I then focus my mind in the present and appreciate what is working today in my life.

I stop suffering over past experiences and appreciate the good in the present moment.

Emotional Reactions

I am aware that my emotional reactions
are bigger than the people or events
that trigger them.

I understand that I react to a pattern built up in
my mind from similar hurtful issues
from my past.

Today, I pay attention to these reactions and ask
myself: "Is this a pattern? When has this rejection
or anger response happened in me before? What
past circumstances feel familiar now? Of whom
does this situation remind me?"

I release the pain of the past by seeing people
and events in the present as triggers and not the
cause of my reactions.

I respond in present time rather than
react to emotional triggers.

---

*I allow people and events to "trigger" me
in order to make peace with my past.*

Value-Judging

I stop finding fault with myself and others.

I pay attention whenever I use "shoulds" and "oughts," as they are value-judgments which lower my self-esteem.

Rather than criticize or judge, I ask myself, "What am I willing to do, or not do, in the future if this situation comes up again?"

Then I take positive risks to move beyond unhealthy old patterns.

I am willing to live with the consequences of these new choices.

*I stop value-judging
myself and others.*

Mistakes

I go easy on myself when I make a mistake, realizing that this is how I learn and grow.

If I had known the outcome of a choice before I made it, then I would have had the awareness to choose differently.

I stop my critical mind when I replay over and over situations that I judge as bad or wrong.

I take time to learn from my mistakes and make amends wherever possible.

I forgive myself for making poor, unaware choices in the past.

*I use my mistakes
to grow in awareness.*

Feelings

My feelings are not right or wrong.

I understand feelings are simply part
of my inner guidance system.

They give me feedback on thoughts
and reactions to my daily experiences and
encounters with others.

I am learning to put words to what I'm feeling,
which helps me identify thoughts and beliefs
behind the feelings.

Once I do this, I use my mind to evaluate these
feelings to best decide what to do next.

Sometimes I simply allow myself to feel my
feelings and sometimes I use them as motivators
to help me make beneficial changes.

I acknowledge all my feelings.

---

*I always tell myself the truth
about what I am feeling.*

Emotional Victim

I give up being an emotional victim, where I feel powerless around people who blame me for their problems or project anger onto me.

I observe the part I play in dramas with others in order to change my part in the scripts.

I remember to turn inward to gather inner strength and connect to my spiritual power.

As I begin assessing an unwanted situation, I release unrealistic expectations and accept people and events that I cannot change.

If necessary, I remove myself from a negative person or situation.

I remember that I can only work on myself.

As I change, I no longer play my role as emotional victim.

I give up being an emotional victim.

Unwanted Behavior

I choose to understand my unwanted behavior
so I can get better results in my life.

I look behind my behavior to discover the
causes, to see my needs and the unwise choices
I make to get them met.

Some of my needs are unconscious to me and
some compete with one another, therefore
causing unwanted behavior at times.

I want clarity so I can change the actions that I
do not want to continue.

I go within and ask my wise inner
Self for clues to this puzzle.

*I have the power to
change unwanted behavior.*

Forgiving Myself

I forgive myself for things I have said, thought, or done in the past that I do not like.

I remind myself that I only did what I could do at the time based on my level of understanding at that time.

It no longer serves me to use today's awareness to judge yesterday's actions.

Today, I know I would do things differently.

I continue to learn from my unwise choices and make amends when appropriate.

I change my negative self-talk with positive affirmations when I find myself mentally "beating myself up."

I forgive myself for unaware things
I have said and done in the past.

Vulnerability

I appreciate that I am an open, sensitive,
and vulnerable person.

I view vulnerability as a strength and an asset.

It allows me to feel deeply, to connect to
others easily on an emotional level,
and to feel more alive.

I pay attention to where I'm vulnerable to the
"not so good" intentions of some people.

I properly protect myself from being taken
advantage of, lied to, or hurt.

I choose to be vulnerable as much of the time as
possible, using my awareness to guide me.

Being vulnerable enriches my relationships,
allowing intimacy and bonding.

---

*I appreciate my vulnerability and stay
aware to properly protect myself.*

Integrity

I choose to live with integrity: being honest
and sincere, a person of my word and of
sound moral character.

I make a list of my values and add to it
as my awareness grows.

The closer I live within my sound value system,
the greater the integrity I have with myself
and then to share with others.

To build integrity, I observe and honestly
evaluate my actions and thoughts
on a regular basis.

I set small goals and take one step at a
time to correct the areas of my life
that need higher integrity.

---

*I strive to live my life
with high integrity.*

Blame

I feel sadness and remorse for unwise choices
that have hurt me or others in the past.

Continually blaming myself with negative
self-talk lowers my self-esteem.

I am, however, responsible for everything
I say, think, and do.

I release patterns of punishing myself with
continual blame or guilt.

When blame comes up, I ask myself, "What can
I learn from this situation that will enable me to
create a different outcome that I will be proud of
next time? How can I make amends
and is it appropriate to do so?"

I forgive myself for unaware choices in the past.

***I stop blaming myself
for unwise choices.***

Releasing Pain

I release emotional pain by journal writing, crying, or talking to a person with a kind ear about my hurt, anger, and depression.

I forgive people, situations, and myself for being unaware and causing me pain.

When I am ready, I detach and see us as characters in a play, acting out parts in a script that was written at an unconscious level of awareness.

I see that the victims and victimizers were both trapped, repeating patterns and not able to realize there are always choices.

Today, I am more aware and choose to forgive so I can move beyond this script.

I release pain from the past by forgiving every person, including myself, for being unaware.

Preferences

I scan my life for areas where I allow myself
to be hurt with expectations set too high.

I understand that expectations that get out of
hand become emotionally charged demands or
emotional addictions that rule me.

I can defuse the power these emotional
addictions have over me by changing
them to preferences.

Preferences are soft and flexible, while
emotional addictions are demands that
are rigid and inflexible.

I change my emotionally backed expectations
to preferences, which allows me the freedom to
flow around unwanted outcomes.

---

*I turn emotional demands
into preferences.*

Goals

Today, I think about my goals and
write down three of them.

I set realistic goals, as standards set too low or
too high lower my good feelings about myself.

I take my three goals and write down several
small steps needed to achieve each.

I allow the proper time frame for me
to achieve my goals.

I evaluate, prioritize, and adjust my goals
periodically because as I change
my goals can change.

*I set realistic goals
for myself.*

Thoughts

My thoughts are powerful and direct my life.

My current thoughts create tomorrow.

Today, I practice identifying some of my thoughts and beliefs in order to update those no longer serving me.

I say affirmations to change my negative thoughts to positive ones.

I plant new seed thoughts in my mind based on love and truth.

I plant healthy, loving thoughts in the garden of my mind.

Boundaries

I pay attention to my physical and emotional
boundaries, the personal space around me.

I notice when I'm in harmony with another.

I notice when I feel uncomfortable
with someone.

I take action to care for myself by setting clear
boundaries that support me having a safe place
both physically and emotionally.

I communicate clearly so others
understand my limits.

I remove myself from situations or people when
my boundaries are not respected.

I stay conscious so that I interact with others in
healthy ways that support my needs.

---

*I set appropriate physical and emotional
boundaries for myself.*

*My Mother**

I love and appreciate my mother.

I am grateful for the gift of life she gave me and the sacrifices she made for me.

All that I learned being her child is a part of me now.

I release and forgive all the judgments and criticisms I have about wanting some things to have been different in my childhood.

I send love and forgiveness to my mother.

My inner mother loves and nurtures me.

** This passage may be read on
your mother's birthday.*

---

*I love and appreciate
my mother.*

Prosperity

I am prosperous.

My prosperity is more than having all the money I want, it grows out of finding fulfillment within myself, my relationships, and all that I do.

I heal lack or scarcity in any area of my life as I focus on building prosperity consciousness.

To create more cash flow, for example, I ask myself where I stop my prosperity with negative attitudes, opinions, or beliefs about having money or deserving money.

I set in motion a plan to spend less than I make, repay old debts even if a long time has passed, save, give to individuals or organizations, and become debt free.

My creativity actualizes unexpected ways to acquire what I want.

***My abundance grows as
I build prosperity consciousness.***

Receiving

I allow receiving into my life.

When another person gives me a compliment or does a kindness for me I easily accept.

Receiving from another builds friendship and connectedness.

I enjoy and appreciate kindness from others.

I balance giving and receiving in my life, as they are different halves of a whole and one without the other is incomplete.

I like to experience both giving and receiving.

I receive graciously.

Giving

I am a giving person and respond appropriately
to the needs of others.

I listen to my inner self to identify what
I need to do for myself, so I have clear
boundaries and know my limits.

I fill myself emotionally and spiritually to make
sure my giving is genuine and from the heart.

I give without an expectation of a return; the
rewards of healthy giving are the good feelings
I receive when expressing kindness toward
another or giving acts of service.

I check my tendency to over-give, which usually
happens when I forget to take care of myself
and give for the wrong reasons: to receive love,
attention, praise, or acknowledgment.

---

*I give freely to others
from my overflow.*

Self-Improvement

I am good even when I have habits, actions, or thinking patterns that I do not like.

Rather than put myself down for these parts of myself that I do not like, I make an improvement plan.

Often, I remind myself of my new intentions and take small steps to transform.

I observe myself as I go through my day, noticing where I can make positive changes in my behavior, speech, thinking, and self-talk.

I go easy on myself and know it takes time to make changes, realizing my good intentions support the process.

To improve my life, I observe people who model positive ways.

I choose continuous self-improvement as a way of life.

Improving a Relationship

I study one of my relationships.

Rather than waste time thinking how I would like the other to be different, I ask, "What can I do differently to change the dance between us?"

My intentions pave the way for my experiences, so I focus on how to improve our relationship.

When conflict arises, I limit my defenses, hear what is spoken and unspoken, and allow new patterns to arise.

I make conscious choices to think, say, and act with an open mind and loving heart.

I improve my relationships by focusing on what I can do differently.

Mirrors

Everyone is my mirror.

I understand myself better by looking at the
reflection others give me.

I would not see something in another if it were
not a part of me or a potential within me.

I remember that everyone is capable of wise and
unwise actions and that I have choices.

Instead of judging others as good or bad, I seek
to learn from everyone I meet.

I notice when another shows me
how I do not want to be.

I spend time with the people who reflect my
goodness, love, and beauty.

---

*I allow the mirrors of others to teach me
about myself and my potential.*

Talents

I feel good about myself when I develop my talents and abilities.

My talents may or may not be achievements highly valued by society.

My gifts may be playing the piano, writing poetry, taking care of plants, working easily with children, playing sports to the best of my abilities, being intuitive with animals, or having the patience to listen to others in need.

I go within and remember the things I like to do and what excites me about life.

It's time again to focus on my talents and gifts so I can express more of myself.

It pleases me to develop and use my talents.

I take one step today to develop and use my talents.

Spiritual Essence

There is much more to me than my
personality, behavior, and mind.

I am a spiritual being that exists
beyond the physical level of life.

As I open my heart and mind I experience
my true nature, my spiritual essence.

I spend quiet time in prayer, meditation,
and contemplation to improve my
connection to my spiritual roots.

*I grow daily in understanding and
expressing my spiritual essence.*

Spiritual Nourishment

Spiritual nourishment is the source
of my inner strength and power.

I open my heart and fill myself with love
and light from The Source.

I imagine golden-white light pouring energy
in and around and through me to nourish my
mind and all the cells of my body.

I feel oneness will all of creation.

My emotional well-being is uplifted
by receiving nourishment from Spirit.

I go into my day empowered, knowing
I have everything I need to handle
what comes up in my day.

---

*I receive spiritual nourishment
and feel whole and complete.*

Purpose

I have a special purpose only I can fulfill.

No one else is exactly like I am, so only I can
fulfill the destiny of being me.

As I learn and grow in consciousness, I become
more aware of my spiritual purpose.

I begin by listening to the still, quiet voice within
on a daily basis.

I am learning to become my true Self and
actualize my purpose.

---

*I have a special purpose and it begins
with self-awareness and learning
to be my own unique self.*

Sacred Space

I create a sacred space in my home where I
meditate, pray, and contemplate my life.

My sacred space could be a room in my home or
a certain chair and table in a quiet corner.

In my sacred space I put my favorite items that
remind me of my spiritual, inner work, such as
favorite books, pictures, and things that make
me happy and feel good.

I keep a journal here to log important insights
and inner experiences.

*I create a sacred space to do my inner
healing work.*

School of Life

I look at life as if it were a school.

I remember that I am here to learn and grow, to become fully aware of who and what I am.

I see the challenges that come my way as part of the curriculum that I signed up for at the spiritual level of my being.

Rather than criticize, deny, or avoid my problems, I see them as opportunities for growth.

I pay special attention to lessons which nourish my well-being: interacting with others to experience love, support, and caring, growing in awareness, developing my gifts and talents, resolving conflict.

I am in the school of life and learn from every experience.

Problems

I look at problems in a new way; they are calling
for my attention and I have a chance
to do things differently.

When I take the time to study issues in my life,
I begin seeing alternatives that were
not obvious at first.

As I gather information on an issue giving me
difficulty, I see there are people who have walked
a similar path before me who are available
to be my teachers.

My problems are no longer traps,
simply a means to becoming more aware.

*I see my problems as
opportunities for growth.*

Valentine

I am my own valentine today.

I say kind things to myself, repeating
my favorite affirmations.

I extend kindness to others by smiling and
making eye contact.

I verbalize my love and appreciation to my
friends and family.

I give a card to special people in my life.

---

*I express love and kindness to others
on Valentine's Day.*

Questioning

I like to think about and prove the validity of
new ideas before making them mine.

I remember to question new ideas that I read in
books or hear from others.

Before blindly accepting new concepts into my
consciousness I like to question
their practical application.

Once I see the benefit of an idea, I then update
my belief system with the new ideas.

I value taking the time to question
new points of view.

---

*I question ideas as I open my mind to
new points of view.*

Love Versus Like

I am aware of the difference between
loving and liking.

I can unconditionally love someone
and not like their character.

My like or dislike of someone is an emotional
response and has a lot to do with
how much we have in common.

Choosing to love everyone does not dictate
any behavior on my part.

Sometimes the most loving thing for me to do
is to not be around someone I do not like, as I
must take care of myself.

I choose to be around people I like.

---

*I choose to love everyone and build
friendships with people I like.*

Intellectualizing

I notice when I'm "in my head" and not participating in my life.

Talking about and analyzing my problems are good to a point; however, my growth stops when I spend too much time intellectualizing.

I now begin taking risks to apply what I know I need to do.

I stop intellectualizing my problems and take positive action.

Wellness

I enjoy wellness.

When off balance, I pay attention to the messages my body gives me in the metaphor of illness, aches, or pain.

For example, a pain in my neck may be telling me to deal with a person with whom I have tolerated too much and need to confront.

As I crack the code of the metaphors, I make positive changes to heal my thoughts, feelings, and actions which influence my health positively.

I also take care of myself on the physical level, practicing healthy habits to promote my health and wellness.

I enjoy wellness and listen when my body talks to me.

Inner Peace

I experience inner peace when I love and
forgive others on a continual basis.

It's predictable that I will get my feelings hurt or
want to defend myself when I allow another to
push my emotional buttons.

In order to change my reactive behavior and
feelings, I go within to center myself with deep
breathing and remind myself that inner peace is
a choice cultivated over time.

I spend time alone each day to
enjoy my inner peace.

I add peace to the world by first experiencing
peace within and then practicing it with others.

*I choose
inner peace.*

Fear

I acknowledge my fear thoughts and feelings, no longer letting them get me down or stop my progress for long.

When irrational thoughts and feelings of fear arise, I feel the fear and keep on taking risks to improve my life.

I change my negative self-talk and pessimistic attitude by overriding them with affirmations of new truths.

I respect a healthy response of fear when I need to take action to remove myself from danger.

I acknowledge my fear and continue taking positive risks.

Assimilating

Sometimes I judge myself as falling behind or failing to grow when I'm at a standstill.

I now know I have reached a plateau, usually after a period of accelerated growth.

A lot takes place internally on these plateaus.

I am assimilating and putting into practice what I have recently learned.

I am committed to my growth path and enjoy the pauses along the way.

I accept the pauses in my life as the perfect time to assimilate new ideas.

Value

I value all life.

I am a valuable part of humanity.

I am worthy and of equal value to every other person; value has nothing to do with differences in abilities, interests, race, education, religious beliefs, or economic level.

I value and accept individual differences among people.

My self-esteem is based on valuing and accepting myself today as I am and striving to build a better me one step at a time.

---

*I value myself and
every other person.*

Approval

I approve of myself and how I live my life.

I stop getting my security and acceptance needs
met from other people's approval.

When others approve of me, I joyfully accept it
in the moment and let go of depending on or
expecting it in the future.

As I learn new values, attitudes, beliefs, and
behaviors, I do not expect others to always
understand or be able to give me their approval.

It's important to allow others
to disagree with me. As the love and support
for myself grows, the need for approval or
agreement from others lessens.

I give myself approval to make positive changes
in my life.

---

*I give myself approval to grow and change,
releasing the need for others' approval.*

Self-Talk

I monitor my self-talk.

When I hear criticism, "shoulds," and "put downs," I override them with positive, encouraging, non judgmental words.

If I hear negative comments from others directed to hurt me, I quickly release them from my mind.

I change my conditioned mind by repeating affirmations to myself often.

I talk kindly to myself with positive self-talk.

Avoidance

Today, I pay attention to what
makes me uncomfortable.

I notice the things I want to avoid.

I pay attention to my body awareness and the
feelings that come up for me when
resistance surfaces.

I choose to stay with the discomfort, knowing it
is showing me something.

I then ponder the meaning behind my thoughts
and feelings when uncomfortable, to determine
what I need to do with the information,
if anything.

Sometimes just being aware of what is taking
place is enough.

---

*I stop avoiding and face what makes me
feel uncomfortable.*

Expectations

I accept where I am on my life-path and
have reasonable expectations for
my growth and healing.

It no longer serves me to expect myself to be
farther along on my journey.

I can only be where I am.

When I catch myself being unrealistic and
expecting too much from myself, I take time
out to center myself, quiet my mind, and begin
saying positive things to myself.

I build my self-esteem by knowing where I am
going and knowing it takes time to put into
practice the new ideas I am learning.

*I let go of expecting too much,
too fast from myself.*

Gratitude

I am grateful for so many things in my life.

I start a gratitude journal to daily list several
things I'm thankful for each day.

I begin today listing happy memories and listing
all the people with whom I feel connected.

I appreciate myself for being open to new ideas
to change my life.

I appreciate my awareness, which helps me see
how to create goodness in my life.

I watch the seeds of gratitude grow daily
in my garden.

*I have an attitude
of gratitude.*

Well-Nourished

I am well-nourished physically, emotionally, socially, mentally, and spiritually because I take good care of myself.

I have a daily routine that includes getting proper rest, eating healthy foods, and exercise that suits my personality.

I nourish myself by decorating with and wearing my favorite colors.

I start or develop a hobby that gives me pleasure and nourishment.

I expose myself to new ideas in books, classes, or lectures to stimulate and nourish my mind.

I am well-nourished because I take excellent care of myself.

Magical Day

Today is a special bonus day.

I allow my inner secret wishes, hopes, and
dreams to surface.

I write them down in my journal
so I remember them.

As I become aware of what I want, this plants
seeds in the garden of my mind of new goals to
strive toward.

*I let the magic of the day show me my
secret wishes, hopes, and dreams.*

Grounding

I begin my day by centering and
grounding myself.

I stand with my feet planted firmly on the
ground and take several deep breaths.

I feel Mother Earth supporting me, feeling safe
and secure in my physical body.

As I remember to connect to this solid place,
I remain centered as I go through the
experiences of my day.

When I am grounded I think more clearly and
make wiser choices that support me.

At any time I lose focus, am accident prone, or
repeatedly make small mistakes, I take a few
moments to think of my feet, deep breathe, and
remember to ground myself.

---

*I ground myself and feel the solid support
of Mother Earth.*

Projection

I stop projecting my issues onto others.

I own the things I see others play out for me that are difficult to own and I take responsibility for working on them within myself.

Each time I judge and see what another could do to improve his or her life, I bring my attention back to myself.

I am the only person I can change and realize I have no control over others.

Each person can act only according to his or her level of awareness and I choose to expand mine in order to grow and heal.

As my power of observation grows, I see where others project their issues on me and I practice detachment.

I stop projecting my issues onto others and do not take it personally when others project onto me.

Everyone Is My Teacher

Today, I remain mindful that
everyone is my teacher.

I choose to learn from all people.

I pay special attention to people whom I react to
or whose behaviors or points of view I dislike, as
they teach me how I choose not to live my life.

I enjoy the teachers who express my goodness
and those who show me the way when I am
confused or lost.

As my power to discriminate increases, I am able
to learn from all people.

I grow by observing what I like and
dislike in all people.

---

*I see everyone as my teacher and use
information from each for refining
my own personality.*

Slowing the Pace

Sometimes I wish I could go back in time
to being less aware, and therefore be less
responsible for my life.

It takes a lot of energy to continually transform
my personality, my actions, and my beliefs.

I know I asked to see all parts of myself and
sometimes it's overwhelming to see
what I do not like.

In reality, I know I cannot return
to being unaware.

I can, however, take a break from the fast track
pace of self-discovery.

I enjoy a pause in growth today,
as a slower pace nurtures me.

---

*I slow the pace of self-discovery today
and enjoy resting.*

One Day at a Time

When I get stressed, feel there is more to do than
I'm prepared to handle, or want to return to a
bad habit or addiction, I remind myself
to live one day at a time.

Pushing myself to do more, to be further along
when I want fast changes, can be frustrating.

I settle down when I remember all I can really
do is live today and do only what I can do today,
one step at a time.

Tomorrow will soon be today and I will repeat
living one day at a time.

It's appropriate to take risks and to set new goals,
but thinking too much about the future robs me
of enjoying today.

---

*I live one day at a time and focus only on
what is appropriate for my growth right now.*

Openness

I open my heart to the love and support
that is in my life.

I open my mind to new ideas and
expand my knowledge.

I release the obstacles and fears from the past
that have impeded my growth.

I trust the process of inner work, growth, and
healing to build openness in my personality.

---

*I open my heart and mind to new
possibilities.*

Inner Female

My wise inner female, or yin side, knows how to love and nurture myself and others.

I turn inward today to feel this quiet power.

I open to listening to the wisdom and insight of my inner female side.

My inner female supports my inner knowing, my inner work, and how to build good relationships with others.

I integrate the gentleness of my inner female into the greater me.

I receive nurturing and guidance from my inner female.

Inner Male

My inner male, or yang side, knows how to encourage and protect me when I go out into the world.

I listen to the wisdom of this part of my consciousness when things get tense and I need to take care of myself.

I transform the places where I do not take proper care of or protect myself.

I tune in to my inner male to help me deal with issues in the workplace.

I draw on the strength of my inner male to guide and protect me in the world.

Journal Writing

I write my thoughts, feelings, and insights
in a journal.

I record my reactions to people and events,
writing letters I do not send to those I have
unresolved anger toward.

I write about my traits, beliefs, issues,
goals, accomplishments, and the lessons
I'm currently working on.

My pain, sadness, anger, hurts, and fears are
eased as I write them down.

I receive clarity for myself and communicate
better when I put what I feel into words.

I write about my feelings of joy, love, peace,
connectedness, and comfort.

---

*I keep a journal to help me process
and integrate my feelings, thoughts,
and experiences.*

Risks

I take one risk today that moves me out of an old, unwanted pattern, habit, or trait.

I watch others who live the way I want to live and who show me new ideas and model the risks I need to take.

It comforts me to find and carry with me a symbol for inner strength, such as an acorn, a rock, crystal, or coin as I step forward.

I focus on my intentions as I take steps to break out of crystallized habits or patterns.

I take a small risk today to build a better tomorrow.

Visualization

I think about what I want to create in my life.

I explore alternative futures with the power of
visualization to see which ones I really
want to manifest.

Once I know what I desire, I visualize often
what that reality would feel like.

I imagine this new reality, enjoying
all the good feelings.

I add power to these pictures by affirming what
I want to manifest.

*I use the power of my mind to visualize
what I want to manifest.*

Information

I gather new information to help me make positive changes in my life.

I read self-help and spiritual books and listen to motivational CD's, as there are many teachers available to me.

As I open my mind to new information, I remember to use my intellect to help me decide whether or not a new concept is wise to incorporate into my belief system.

I notice whether the ideas help me gain clarity about my life, my issues, my thinking, my behavioral tendencies, and my relationships.

If so, the new information becomes mine.

I gather new information to expand my awareness.

Time Alone

I spend time alone daily, as I realize it's one of my basic needs and the way I get to know myself.

I spend at least half an hour each day to observe, ponder, daydream, journal write, meditate, and pray.

Time alone calms and centers me so I can live my life the way I choose and make the changes that support my growth.

Quality alone time is a gift to myself.

I enjoy being with myself.

I feel the power of simply being.

I enjoy quality time alone with myself each and every day.

Healthy People

I spend time with emotionally healthy people who reflect my inner beauty, love, and light.

I choose to be around healthy people who are growing and working on improving themselves.

Healthy people model and reinforce the positive changes manifesting in my life.

This consciousness supports me when I work or live with unaware people.

I spend time with emotionally healthy people who reflect my wholeness.

Meaning

My life has meaning.

I find meaning and purpose in all that I do.

I look for deeper meaning behind unwanted experiences and behavior — mine and other people's — to understand the causes for my problems.

I am like a detective investigating the parts I play, at the unconscious level, in these experiences so that I can make choices to do things differently.

I look for ways to create new outcomes and find new meaning in my life.

---

*I look for meaning
in all my experiences.*

Courage

I have the courage to take another step toward
fully loving and accepting myself.

I allow old feelings of devaluing myself
to come to the surface.

After feeling them, I release them.

New feelings of lightness and aliveness
flow into me.

My future looks bright because I have the
courage to be my real, authentic Self and to take
the risks necessary to create my life
the way it pleases me.

---

*I have the courage to move forward
on my inner journey.*

Confidence

I am growing daily in my confidence.

I am like an acorn growing into my
full-grown-tree self.

Some of my early branches are barren
and stunted and now it's time to grow more
branches and gain fuller stature.

I now have a strong branch of confidence
on my oak tree.

I feel confident and comfortable expressing
publicly who I have grown to become.

My confidence supports me to take risks that
develop inner balance and wholeness.

*I am confident
being me.*

Process

I understand now that life is a process with continual stages of growth and awareness.

I trust that the process of self-discovery and inner healing is taking me to a better place.

I am learning a new language in which I go deeper in understanding myself, using my body awareness, my intuition, and my intellect in new ways to unlock hidden meaning in situations.

I release all unnecessary fear as I move forward trusting my process to improve my life.

---

*I trust the process
unfolding in my life.*

Nature

Nature nurtures me.

I take time daily to fill my soul with deep peace,
comfort, and beauty as I connect to the earth
and its entire splendor.

A moment of standing in sunlight or feeling the
wind on my face stills my mind and empowers
me to move forward in my day.

I enjoy the variety of plants, trees, flowers,
birds, and animals.

I appreciate the rhythm of the change of seasons
and the movement from day to night.

I love the color and dynamics of the sky.

I feel the power behind the beauty and
mystery of nature.

---

*I allow nature to nurture me, still my
mind, and align my spirit.*

Aging

I accept the process of aging in my life.

I know I am much more than my physical body and physical appearance.

I love and accept my body at each age and stage.

I take excellent care of my physical body.

I let go of expecting to be any age other than my current age and ignore the media's emphasis on youth and beauty.

I like the wisdom that builds with age.

---

*I age gracefully
and enjoy my current age.*

Spring Equinox

I celebrate the beginning of spring.

It's a time of rebirth in nature and symbolically in my own life.

I plant new seed thoughts in my mind with positive affirmations and visualizations.

I know I have the proper nutrients to allow them to sprout and grow to fruition.

One nutrient is my commitment to use my new awareness to fertilize the seed thoughts.

Another is taking quiet time each morning to think about and prepare for my day and then in the evening to review my day, looking for ways to make improvements for my future.

I celebrate the spring equinox which symbolizes a rebirth within me.

Deserving

I deserve to live my life with love, joy, peace, health, abundance, and happiness.

I deserve autonomy to make my own choices.

I deserve good relationships.

I release experiences that taught me to believe anything different.

I feel the warmth and power of loving myself.

I am capable of creating my life in ways that fulfill me.

I deserve love, happiness, and fulfillment in my life.

Inner Strength

I feel strong within now.

My inner strength grows daily
as I grow in awareness.

I have the courage and inner strength to meet
all experiences drawn into my day.

I remember to love and honor myself often
as I fill myself spiritually with a
silent prayer or affirmation.

As I center myself and feel solid in my physical
form, I meet my day prepared, full of strength
and confidence.

*I am strong within; and my inner strength
carries me easily through the day.*

Relaxation

I allow my body to relax at the end of the day.

I clear my mind and calm myself with things such as a walk by myself, meditating, taking a hot bath, or doing stretching exercises like yoga.

Anytime during the day that I'm stressed I pause and do this simple relaxation exercise: I slowly breathe in and say in my mind, "One," and then I breathe out and say, "Two." I do this several times.

When I have trouble sleeping I say to myself, "relax, release, easy," over and over as I deep breathe.

I enjoy my relaxation time each day.

Masks

I let go of wearing masks that hide my true Self.

These masks served me earlier in my life; they were the only defenses I knew to use in order to survive.

My protection now comes from my awareness.

I can still choose to wear a mask during times when I feel the need to protect myself and know no other options — I do it consciously now, however.

I no longer fear rejection from others and it cannot manipulate me into masking my true, authentic Self for long.

My public self matches my private self as I feel happy being me.

---

*I remove the masks
that hide the true me.*

True Power

I am in control of my life and I claim
the power to be me.

I act from my own authority and use my
power wisely, not dominating others or
allowing others to overpower me.

I use my power to manifest changes
I truly want.

I know my true power is to align with my
spiritual base.

*I align with my true power,
my spiritual power.*

Loving Kindness

I choose to live my life with loving kindness,
showing others respect, a kind ear,
and understanding.

Even though I may appear to be soft and
vulnerable at times, I have strength from deep
within that helps me set appropriate
boundaries with others.

I choose these boundaries with awareness
so my open heart knows my limits.

Sometimes the most kind and loving thing to do
is confront another, at other times it is to remain
silent, and at other times to simply
acknowledge and affirm.

*I show others the loving kindness
I give myself.*

Happiness

Happiness grows daily in my life, as I live creatively and with awareness.

I feel happy when I honor myself, do my inner healing work, take risks to meet my goals, connect with friends and loved ones, and live my life with meaning and purpose.

My happiness is not dependent on others; it comes from within myself and what I do for myself.

I listen to my unhappy feelings when they arise, as they show me what is "off" in my life and what is needed to get myself back on track.

Quiet time alone to think or journal write, or talking with a close friend lightens my mood and reminds me how to be in charge of my happiness again.

I am
a happy person.

Opportunities

I look for open doors and take opportunities
to meet my goals when they appear.

I experience unexpected inspiration and
motivation to move forward when an
opportunity arises.

I accept positive results and
answers to my prayers.

I notice when limitations are removed
and I break out of old patterns and
easily make progress.

*I appreciate the many opportunities to
change my life and be successful in all I do.*

Enjoyment

I pay attention to the simple things in life
that give me enjoyment.

Today, I choose to enjoy my day, even if
something unexpected comes along that throws
me off center.

One difficult moment does not ruin
my whole day.

I make a list of things I enjoy.

I do one thing each day that brings me pleasure
and enjoyment.

I choose to enjoy my day.

The Journey

I see my life as an exciting journey.

I transform all that no longer serves me
into a life that I love.

The journey is a process and day by day
I move along learning and growing.

I find enjoyment in today's part of the journey
and do not focus only on the goal.

Life is a process which I enter into freely.

I accept the journey that is my life.

---

*I accept the journey of life in all its
richness of experiences, lessons,
and processes.*

Playfulness

I enter the day with the intention to play.

I look for ways to laugh as I celebrate
April Fool's Day.

I really pay attention when a child or
friend plays a joke on me.

I laugh and I lighten up, as it's a
day to be playful.

My inner child looks for simple ways
to play, joke, and have fun.

*I am playful
and like to laugh.*

Growth

I am like a seedling growing to fruition in the soil of experience.

I fertilize the seedling with new ideas, affirmations, and visualizations.

It's never too late to grow deeper roots and build a stronger foundation for my life.

I continue to change my self-talk to a kind, loving, and supportive voice to help me grow into a fully-functioning person.

I grow daily into a fuller expression of myself.

Goodness

Goodness operates in my life.

I am worthy of experiencing
good things in my life.

I am good even if my behavior, thinking, or
communication with others needs
some improvement.

I separate my behavior from the real me so I can
know and feel my innate goodness.

I spread goodness in the world by sharing with
others what I have and what I have learned.

*I notice goodness
throughout my day.*

Self-Care

I appreciate that I am growing in many new ways, including self-care.

I look for ways to take better care of myself, such as, proper sleep, diet, exercise, emotionally connecting with others, learning new ideas, and broadening my spiritual perspective.

I take responsibility for meeting many of my own needs and desires.

I notice today where I need attention.

As I nurture the part of me that is in the most need today, my whole being benefits.

I practice self-care daily in order to stay balanced and productive.

This nurturing supports my growth.

---

*I take care of myself on all levels —
physically, emotionally, socially,
mentally, and spiritually.*

Perfect Order

My life is in perfect order.

At each stage in my growth and development,
I am perfecting being who I am capable
of being at the time.

I can only do what I am able to do at each stage
based on my current awareness.

I release critical self-talk that expects more than
I can currently deliver.

I understand that I need to integrate all that I
have learned before new information is available
for me to understand.

---

*I trust my life is unfolding
in perfect order.*

Challenges

Life challenges open my eyes to unconscious aspects of myself and give me the opportunity to grow in awareness.

Without resistance and challenge, I would not notice or pay attention to undeveloped parts of myself.

I grow as I undergo a life challenge, such as an illness, a relationship problem, or a career or job challenge.

Though I may find some parts of the passage difficult, I remain mindful in order to grow in awareness.

I accept life challenges as opportunities for my growth and awareness.

My Body

I love my body and my body loves me.

I take care of my body to build a strong vessel so I can easily fulfill my purpose.

I work from where my body is presently, not comparing myself to a perfect ideal, other people, or to myself in the past.

I get my hair cut regularly, receive dental and eye care, and schedule appropriate medical and chiropractic appointments.

I care about my body and do nurturing things to support my well-being.

*My body is my friend and
I take care of my body.*

Inner Vision

I am developing my inner vision to see beyond
the obvious in my life circumstances.

My intuition gives me insights that
my five senses do not pick up.

I use this vision wisely and with good intentions
to better understand myself, situations, and
people, to help others, or to solve problems.

I expand my inner vision to help me see what is
really going on in situations that feel "off."

Tuning in to my inner vision helps empower me
to take good care of myself and to not be naive.

---

*I trust my inner vision to protect
and guide me.*

Evolving

I experience my life evolving into greater
harmony, with deeper meaning and purpose.

Everything I think, feel, and do gives me the
opportunity to explore deeper to discover ways
to evolve my consciousness.

Today, I notice the unity of all life and
feel my place in it.

I concentrate on the places where humanity is
evolving and add my weight to the collective
experience with my good intentions, healing
thoughts, and right actions.

---

*I am evolving and growing daily in
harmony and wholeness.*

Self-Esteem

I feel my worth, know I am of value,
and that my life counts.

I love and accept myself today as I am,
even as I grow and evolve.

My self-esteem is now based on an inner locus
(center) of control and not on the hurtful words
or actions of unaware people.

I no longer compare myself with anyone and feel
I am a valuable member of the human family
and all of Life.

I accept Divine Love into my life.

*I allow Divine Love to flow into my life
and fuel my self-esteem.*

My Life

I love my life.

I appreciate my life and the
opportunity to be alive.

I see the beauty and splendor of my life.

My life is important and I make a difference.

Daily, I step further on my path to discover
more about myself and explore all the choices
available to me.

I have fun becoming all I was created to be.

I see the importance of simply being myself and
am grateful to live my life the way I choose.

*I am at peace with myself and
how I live my life.*

Perfection

Today, I look at the perfection of my life, which includes all the imperfections.

I am like an oak tree growing from an acorn into greater degrees of maturity, perfect at each stage of growth.

I accept each stage of my growth and development without judgment.

I appreciate the beauty and perfection of my life.

I am perfect at each stage of my development along my life's journey.

Perseverance

I have perseverance to stay in the running until
the end of a healing process.

I stay fully present to acknowledge and respond
to a problem, crisis, or a life challenge.

When I feel like giving up, I remind myself
that avoiding or denying keeps me stuck and
unaware, re-experiencing unnecessary pain.

I have determination now to avoid the surprise
of hidden agendas that pop up when I do not
deal with an issue.

Instead, I gather information, take the risks
necessary to meet my challenges,
and deal with them.

---

*I have the perseverance to transform my
problems and challenges.*

Knowing Self

I am the person I spend the most time with,
so it's important to know myself.

It's not selfish to spend time learning to
know who I am.

I take the time to discover what my thoughts,
beliefs, feelings, values, goals, and needs are.

When I know myself, I avoid being manipulated
by others or by life's circumstances.

I prepare myself for increasing success by
knowing myself well.

*I spend time
getting to know myself.*

Poor Me

I pay attention when I slip back into old,
dysfunctional patterns of playing the
script of poor me.

I no longer pass the buck and place blame on
another when I'm having a difficult time, even if I
can get agreement from others that I'm a victim.

I no longer need sympathy or attention for being
in a negative situation, because it stops
my growth and keeps me stuck playing
the old poor me script.

I accept empathy from others who have
compassion for me when a difficult situation
shows up in my life.

It empowers me to be proactive in changing
victim patterns, to see what I need to do
differently to get new results.

*I claim responsibility for improving my
life and stop playing poor me.*

Communication

In communicating with others, I balance my listening with my talking.

If either is lacking, I miss a chance to have equal, reciprocal relationships.

When in conflict with someone, I really focus when s/he is speaking so I can pick up more than the words spoken and hear the real message.

As I share openly and honestly, others can understand and be there for me.

I balance my listening and talking when communicating to others.

Consequences

I have the power to think, speak,
or act in any way I choose.

I always pay the consequences, however.

Some consequences have good results and
therefore teach me what I want to repeat
in future situations.

Other consequences have negative results and
show me what I choose not to repeat.

I choose my thoughts, words, and actions with
awareness to get the results I want.

*I allow the consequences of my words,
thoughts, and behaviors to be my teachers.*

Patterns

I choose to see and understand the patterns that repeat themselves in my life.

I allow painful patterns from my early life to surface so that I can release feelings of powerlessness and grieve the pain and loss.

Once I see a pattern repeating in the present (the people may be different but the circumstances are similar), I then use my free-will choice to do something different from my instinctual response.

I acknowledge the positive patterns easily operating in my life, as well.

I build awareness of myself by identifying patterns in my life.

Repressed Feelings

I allow repressed feelings of anger, sadness, hurt, rejection, or depression to surface.

I let go of the power they have over me.

In meditation, I surround myself with love and light, breathe deeply, and bring forth one situation from the past that needs to be healed, resolved, understood, or accepted.

I ask my higher Self to guide me as I review the situation through new eyes, allowing the process of forgiveness to heal the effects of the past.

To process these feelings I journal write or walk outside to receive the healing power of nature.

I seek outside help if I need more support.

I allow repressed feelings to surface in order to transform them into the light of understanding and forgiveness.

Resolving Issues

I notice any emotional outbursts or strong
reactions I have today.

I know they are clues to the unconscious issues
that I have yet to resolve from the past.

I ask myself how the current person or situation
reminds me of a past situation.

As I do this, I find it easier and easier to forgive
the current situation and to have a healthy
response based on current feelings and reactions.

---

*I use my emotional reactions to resolve
and forgive issues from the past.*

Asking

I ask for what I need and want.

If it involves others, I allow each to respond as
she or he chooses or is able.

I do not coerce another into pleasing me
and I receive only what another is capable of
giving, if anything.

I open my mind and heart to new and different
ways of receiving.

Sometimes I may have to wait for proper timing,
do more inner work to remove my blocks to
receiving, or I may need to take a risk to do
something new.

I watch as my creativity soars, showing me ways
to manifest what I want. I am open to receiving
in unexpected ways.

---

*I ask and
doors open to receive.*

Inner Resistance

I watch my inner resistance to people and
experiences by noticing my emotional reactions,
as well as tension in my body.

I deep breathe to quiet my mind
and feel centered.

I open my heart and practice unconditional
love and forgiveness.

When resisting others' unwanted behaviors
and points of view, I remember to practice being
non-judgmental and release
unrealistic expectations.

I release resistance within myself that stops me
from creating my life the way I deserve.

*I practice tolerance and understanding
and my inner resistance dissolves.*

Excitement

I find it's important to find some excitement in each day so I will enjoy my life.

I pay attention to the things that ignite my interest in life.

Feeling excitement gives me feedback on the things that are stimulating to me.

I pay attention to my inner needs to determine whether I need more or less excitement in my day.

I am excited about my day and notice the things that bring me joy.

Being Open

I practice being open with myself
and others today.

I easily connect to others when I stay open.

My intuition gives me feedback on how much
to reveal in each situation, as it is sometimes
unwise to be too open.

I recognize when I'm too open with others who
do not have my best interest at heart.

My protection is my awareness and ability to
foresee consequences.

*I enjoy the fruits of being open
with myself and others.*

Enmeshment

I notice when I lose a sense of self and get caught up in other people's dramas.

I stop making others feel better at the expense of not taking care of my own emotional needs.

I empathize with others, yet detach from feeling too deeply or solving the problems of those I care about.

I avoid enmeshment into other people's problems and emotional dramas.

Balance

I strive for balance within myself and
in my relationships with others.

I pay attention to my needs and wants, observing
how they affect the people around me.

I choose to balance my needs with the needs of
the people with whom I live and work.

When in conflict, I determine, to the best of my
ability, who has the greater need at the time so
that this person (whether it's me or not)
can receive first.

I choose not to dominate or be dominated.

The balance of give-and-take is important in my
close relationships.

---

*I balance my needs
with the needs of others.*

Right Action

I tune in to my inner, true Self to determine what
is right for me to do in difficult situations
I experience in life.

When unclear, I go to a quiet place to
contemplate the situation and my choices, and
then I am able to see beyond my emotional and
defensive reactions.

No one can tell me what I should do; they can
only tell me what they might do
in my situation.

I get clear with myself on what my motives are
for any action, so that right action will follow.

*I allow right action
to flow through me.*

Wise Use of Power

I pay attention to how I use my power.

I notice if I feel powerless or powerful.

I empower and balance myself with kind
and loving self-talk so that I can
use my power wisely.

If I dominate and force my will on another,
I notice and make amends.

In learning to use my power wisely, I may make
mistakes and experience extremes sometimes.

For example, if I have had a tendency to be
passive and hold back on my power, I may
overdo assertiveness at first, or vice versa.

Observing myself helps me be better able to
make wise corrections.

---

*I use my power
wisely.*

Good Intentions

I choose to live my life with good intentions, to be compassionate, loving, and kind.

Living from good intentions of love and kindness does not mean I'm a doormat and does not dictate any specific behavior.

Sometimes the most compassionate thing to do is listen to another, sometimes to remove myself from a situation or even confront another, and sometimes to love from afar through prayer and meditation.

As I focus my intentions on loving kindness, right action follows.

It's important to practice this on myself, as well as on others.

I live with good intentions, which allows right action to flow through me.

Encouragement

I am an encouraging, supportive friend.

I give myself encouragement, as well, to continue my path of self-discovery and to do the inner work necessary to heal myself.

I talk gently but firmly to myself as I encourage myself to move forward on my journey.

I encourage myself to take positive risks to change my unwanted patterns of thinking and behaving, even though it may feel unfamiliar and uncomfortable at times.

My close friends appreciate my encouragement.

I like to encourage my friends and myself to take another step forward.

Honoring Myself

I humbly honor myself today.

I respect and appreciate the beauty and perfection of who I am.

I treat myself with the love and respect that I show to others.

It's a privilege to have this life and to creatively express who I am.

I am quietly content being me.

I read this passage often today to counterbalance negative self-talk to the contrary.

I honor myself with respect, love, and reverence.

Body Awareness

I listen to the awareness of my body today.

My body gives me signals when something is off
within myself, with other people,
or in my environment.

I slow down when I notice body cues, such as my
stomach feeling tight or nauseous, a headache, a
pain in my neck, or my palms sweating, knowing
there are messages here to decipher.

I take deep breaths periodically throughout the
day to release tension and stress. This helps me
perceive the messages my body communicates.

*I listen to the wisdom of my
body's awareness.*

Evaluating Myself

Today, I give myself an evaluation.

I take stock of how I'm doing in meeting my goals, taking risks, expressing my value system, and living with integrity.

I notice how far I have traveled in awareness and celebrate the little changes of my progress.

I allow feelings of disappointment or failure to surface, using them for the motivation to begin anew.

I stop measuring myself against unrealistic standards or the expectations of other people.

I am satisfied with myself today.

I honestly evaluate myself and celebrate my progress.

Power to Choose

I have the power to choose my thoughts and behavior and to modify my personality traits.

Today, I choose one thought, behavior, or trait that I am determined to confront and change.

I talk gently, yet firmly, to myself in order to change thoughts of fear and doubt that keep me stuck in old patterns to those of trust and encouragement.

I use affirmations and visualizations to repattern myself and then I feel strongly and deeply as if the change is already true.

I have the power to choose my thoughts and behaviors and to modify my personality traits.

Protection

I feel protection from Spirit.

I pay attention to my feelings, my inner voice, my body awareness, my inner vision, and my intuition as they guide and protect me.

I combine these inner senses with my intelligence to assess new situations and people, to determine whether or not they are safe for me to get involved with.

I no longer naively believe everything I hear from others. I trust my inner knowing first.

I listen to all my guidance systems for safety and protection.

Focus

As I begin my day I focus on required tasks, staying present even when performing simple tasks such as making my bed or making a phone call.

During meditation or time alone I focus on the things I want to create in my life and where I'm headed.

I am honest with myself, acknowledging my private and sometimes hidden desires.

I focus specifically on one thing I want to accomplish and begin moving in that direction.

Small focused steps take me to new places.

I focus on what I want,
which moves me in that direction.

Emotional Strength

I feel emotionally strong.

I know that no matter what happens to me or
what other people say or do, it cannot take away
my inner strength and knowing that I am a
valuable person.

I have control over my inner life and
that empowers me.

I gain emotional strength by connecting to Spirit
and realizing my innate worth and goodness.

*I have
emotional strength.*

Daily Goals

I feel good when I organize my day by listing the goals I wish to accomplish each morning.

This list of daily goals includes quiet time to think and work on my inner growth and healing.

I respond to my physical, emotional, and social goals, as well.

I enjoy the times when I move quickly to accomplish my daily goals.

It nurtures me to manage my time.

I set daily goals
to use my time wisely.

Making a Difference

My life counts in the grand scheme of things.

I know I make a difference and that my job is simply to know, to love, and be my true Self.

I play my part well and know that no one else can take my place.

I allow my inner awareness to guide me to people and places where I can use my gifts and talents to make a better world.

I pursue possibilities and take risks to get involved where I can contribute.

---

*I make a difference
in creating a better world.*

Being Genuine

I am genuine and authentic in my
interactions with others.

Only I can know for sure what my intentions are.

I understand that sometimes another will
misinterpret even the best of my intentions.

I am sincere and honest with myself and let go
of false pretenses because I value being genuine
with each person I talk to.

I choose to relate from the heart
of my authentic being.

---

*I am genuine and authentic in all my
encounters with others.*

Helping Others

I like helping others.

I set clear boundaries and stay aware of my limits and my own needs and wants.

I notice when I forget to take care of myself and give for the wrong reasons: to receive love, attention, praise, or acknowledgment.

I fill myself emotionally and spiritually so that I have the right energy when helping others.

I take care of myself so that I can give appropriately to others, paying attention to what is truly helpful.

I respond with awareness to the needs and wants of others when helping them.

I like to help others and serve from my abundant overflow.

Love

I know love is what life is about.

I deserve love and allow love from my Higher
Power to fill me continuously.

I am growing daily in loving
and accepting myself.

I feel joyful that as love grows within me,
I can easily love others.

I honor the loving spirit in every other person I
meet, no matter how hidden from view.

I graciously receive love from my
close family and friends.

*I am a loving person who gives and
receives love easily.*

Authority of My Soul

Eventually, I have to listen to the wisdom and
agenda of my soul.

The sooner I acknowledge and align
with my spiritual agenda, the sooner
I experience deep peace.

As I break out of old patterns and am growing
into greater awareness, I am free to understand
my purpose in life.

When I listen to the messages of my soul, my life
really gets easier — whether or not people and
situations in my outer world change.

I easily find my way through the rough passages,
gaining wisdom and awareness.

I enjoy the pleasant surprises
as my soul guides me.

---

*I listen to the
authority of my soul.*

Curiosity

I am curious about everything around me.

I want to understand everything I can.

I continuously learn about myself when I allow my curiosity to look for deeper meaning each time challenging people, events, feelings, thoughts, and reactions show up in my life.

I nurture my curious nature.

My curiosity takes me into realms of greater understanding and higher consciousness.

I enjoy and nurture my curiosity.

Open-Minded

I open my mind to new ideas outside of my frame of reference.

Being open-minded allows a new set of possibilities to enter my life.

As I open my mind to experience what my teachers model to me, obstacles disappear from my path.

I expand my awareness easily and quickly when I am open-minded.

I like to listen to new points of view.

I am open-minded and allow new opportunities to flow into my life.

Contribution

I contribute to those around me and choose to
be of greater service to humanity.

I choose to give back, which keeps the cycle of
giving and receiving flowing in my life.

I automatically give by being in a positive state of
mind as I go through my day.

I realize I make a contribution to someone's day
even with a smile or kind word.

It's just as important to reply kindly to the
grocery checker as it is to join a
humanitarian organization.

I contribute to a better world when I give others
respect and kindness.

---

*I contribute to the well-being of others
with respect and kindness.*

Shame

I feel remorse when I do something wrong.

When appropriate, I make amends to others when I have made a mistake, gone against my moral code, or hurt another.

I release unresolved feelings of shame and such beliefs as, "I am a mistake."

I release family and religious patterns of shame passed on to me.

I forgive people who raised me with toxic shame, understanding they treated me as they treated themselves.

I release all feelings of shame for who I am or embarrassment for my needs and wants.

I know I am good and I stop perpetuating family and societal shame.

I release
feelings of toxic shame.

Motivation

I am motivated to improve my life.

I study and learn new ways of thinking in order to keep going when times are rough.

I use the power of my mind to see possibilities that will benefit me.

I picture different scenarios and their consequences to help me determine which feel right to manifest.

I add the power of affirmations to further direct me.

Once I see, feel, and affirm a future that excites and benefits me, I automatically have the motivation to move forward.

---

*I am motivated
to move forward.*

Real Needs

I go within to determine my real needs.

I may have been conditioned by others to strive only for success, recognition, popularity, and achievement.

Thus, I may have missed learning about a whole set of inner needs that are my real needs.

My deeper needs may be to have more alone time, to ponder life's mysteries, to study a subject I value, to repeat affirmations that heal me, to read, to journal write, or to spend time connecting with a supportive friend.

I go within to discover my real needs and make healthy choices to meet these needs.

My Shadow

I pay attention to traits in others that I dislike
or of which I feel envious.

I understand that whatever I disown in myself,
both good and bad, shows up in the mirrors
of other people.

By owning my shadow side (parts of myself that
I do not recognize and have made unconscious
to myself), I take more responsibility for my life.

My power of choice increases when I stop
projecting my shadow onto others.

*I embrace all parts of myself,
including my shadow side.*

Well-Being

I deserve and allow myself to feel good.

I take care of myself and am responsible
for my own well-being.

I have a positive sense of well-being based on all
the wise choices I am making to improve my life.

I do my best at each moment in all situations.

I experience deep peace as I choose a positive
outlook on life, which makes me feel good.

My sense of trust and well-being propels me
forward to experience life to the fullest.

*I enjoy my sense of
well-being.*

Weighing Consequences

I make choices today by looking at the
probable outcomes.

I weigh the consequences of each choice to
determine the wisest choice for me.

If I am willing to pay the consequences, then I
am free to make a choice.

I take responsibility for my choices,
both wise and unwise.

*I make wise choices by weighing
consequences before I act.*

Self-Inquiry

I take time each day to look within,
to question, to ponder.

I ask, "Who am I?"

Then I ask, "Who is the one
asking the question?"

Self-inquiry takes me beyond the personality
and concerns of my little self.

It connects me in a profound way to
something greater.

I rise to the calling of the Greater Me.

I gain comfort in knowing I am much more than
a person struggling to find my way.

---

*I awaken and grow in awareness by
practicing self-inquiry.*

Gentle Strength

I use my gentle strength to move forward today.

I take note of situations I need to confront,
remembering to use my gentle strength.

I stop pushing and shoving to achieve results.

I use my power wisely to get what I want and
need, being assertive and not aggressive.

When I feel overpowered by something or
someone, I call forth my gentle power
to achieve results.

I use my communication skill to resolve conflict,
remembering to curb my reactions, not to place
blame, to listen, and to speak from my
own experience.

---

*I use my gentle strength
when I respond to others.*

Inner Freedom

Knowing myself builds inner freedom.

Understanding why I do certain things
empowers me to improve my life and
solve my problems.

My inner freedom grows as I take charge of my
thoughts, attitudes, and interpretation
of life events.

My inner freedom allows me to watch myself
when interacting with others — to disengage
from drama, move toward inner peace, and build
fulfilling relationships with others.

*I have inner freedom because I know
myself and take charge of my life.*

Humility

I am humble and live with humility.

I acknowledge myself for the courage it is taking to deeply know myself.

I am honest with myself, seeing my good and not-so-good behavior and traits.

I choose to be humble and quiet about loving and respecting myself.

I no longer need to have my looks, good deeds, or accomplishments acknowledged by others in order to feel good.

I take private joy in living my life with quiet humility.

*I live my life
with quiet humility.*

Judgmental

I release being judgmental and critical toward others.

I am secure in my own beliefs and values and have no need to impose them on anyone who disagrees with me.

I stop judging others and let each live by their own code of values and allow each to learn from the consequences of choices.

I notice in my mind when the old pattern of wanting to control another to think, act, or believe as I do comes up.

This gives me the opportunity to fine-tune my progress in releasing being judgmental.

I stop being critical toward myself.

I catch myself when being judgmental and stop.

Physical Health

I take care of my physical health and well-being.

No matter how good my intentions are to improve my life, to take risks, to emotionally feel good, I can only do so to the degree that my physical health is strong and my body is well.

I notice imbalances in my physical health and begin correcting them.

I choose one thing today to begin improving my physical health.

I take small steps to improve my physical health.

Mother/Father/Mentor

I celebrate being a mother/father to my children
or others whom I have mentored.

The joy of impacting another soul enlivens me
and gives my life deep meaning.

I am honored to have the special privilege and
purpose to positively influence another.

I forgive myself when some of my good
intentions were not wise enough at the time and
negatively impacted another.

I know I did my best at the time
based on my awareness.

I visualize myself improving upon a past
situation, seeing my current awareness positively
affecting the other person.

---

*I enjoy being a good
mother/father/mentor.*

Memorial Day

I pay tribute to people who died in wars
protecting the freedom of others.

I forgive the level of awareness of the collective
unconsciousness that uses physical violence to
settle disagreements, conflicts,
and power struggles.

I add peace to our planet by solving my
personal conflicts and power-struggles, learning
conflict resolution techniques, practicing good
communication skills, and loving, respecting,
and empowering others.

I believe when each of us feels safe, loved, and
empowered, the world will no longer need
to use physical force or settle disputes with
authoritarian means.

---

*I solve my conflicts in nonviolent ways
to promote peaceful coexistence.*

Survival

I am a survivor and have overcome many obstacles and challenges.

I am okay because of my spiritual foundation.

I know I am capable of surviving difficult passages in the future because I survived my past.

I am proud of my ability to manage the ups and downs of my life and know it will continue.

I have the power now to attract people, information, and experiences that help me willingly face my life challenges and feel positive about my future.

I am a survivor and feel safe and positive about my future.

Conditioning

I acknowledge both the positive and the negative effects of my childhood conditioning.

I am recovering well from the negative effects of my conditioned past.

I am now strong within and I have the tools and supportive people in my life to speed positive change.

Energy that was blocked because of living from fear, doubt, pain, or separation is now flowing.

I see things from a larger perspective, which ensures I do not get caught in the web of the negative conditioning.

I have gained insights from everything in my early conditioning.

I am at peace with all aspects of my early conditioning.

New Ideas

I plant new ideas or seed thoughts in my mind.

I focus on inspirational ideas that move me in the direction of healing and wholeness.

A simple test to help me recognize this positive direction is to notice whether a certain teaching makes me feel lighter and hopeful, more connected to myself or whether it makes me feel heavy and fearful, more disconnected from myself.

I trust my inner knowing to guide me.

I plant healthy seed thoughts in the garden of my consciousness.

I plant new ideas in the garden of my mind that inspire me to grow and change in positive ways.

Nourishment

I fertilize and water new ideas planted in the garden of my mind.

I nourish my mind with positive affirmations that upgrade my faulty beliefs.

I repeat new seed thoughts over and over until they become second nature to me.

I passionately visualize the outcomes I want in my new life and feel the joy of these scenarios.

I further nourish myself by taking self-discovery workshops, continuing to read self-help books, and being around people who support and reflect beauty, love, and truth to me.

I give myself proper nourishment to flourish.

Integration

I am integrating all my experiences, beliefs, and behaviors to be part of my awareness.

I own all aspects of myself.

I listen to and accept all parts of myself, especially the ones holding on to the past, are fearful, or are blocking my enjoyment of life.

I listen to competing and immature aspects of myself so they will feel understood.

I love these unhealed parts of myself so they will feel safe to mature and move forward — to cooperate on the same team — the team that is Me.

I integrate all aspects of myself to feel whole and complete.

Organization

I organize my life on all levels.

I begin with the mundane by cleaning out my closets, drawers, and my car.

I release items that no longer serve me.

If I do not use or like some of my clothing or possessions, I give them away.

I take the time to grieve when I release items to which I feel overly emotionally attached.

I next look at how I use my time, giving myself permission to eliminate activities and even relationships that do not support my growth and well-being.

I organize my day to include personal growth time as well as time for things I must do.

I organize my possessions and time to feel free and light.

Life-Style Changes

I take a mental inventory today, noticing areas
of my life in which I need to make a permanent
change of habit.

I make a list of the new behaviors desired
and I use them as goals.

A life-style change is a process that takes time
and vigilance, so I give myself the courtesy of
time to take small steps to progress
a little each day.

I read my list of goals often to impact my
subconscious mind.

I remember that the more strongly I feel a desire
for a life-style change and visualize it often, the
faster I create it.

---

*I choose permanent life-style changes that
support my new level of awareness.*

Resistance

I notice when I resist people, ideas, suggestions,
or my inner wisdom.

I slow down and listen to my fears and doubts
when I'm unable to make a change or a decision
to move forward.

I honor these resistances as they show me where
I need to spend time looking at unconscious
blocks or competing needs that are going in
opposite directions.

I can only progress as fast as I understand and
work with my resistances.

*I learn from
what I resist.*

Spiritual Guidance

I ask for spiritual guidance to help me
over the rough spots in my life.

The answers may come from direct experience,
through meditation, from a book, a TV show, or
from another person.

I am receptive to receiving help and answers
when I call for guidance.

*I receive spiritual guidance
whenever I ask for assistance.*

Humor

I use humor daily.

When I take myself too seriously, I miss enjoying the moment by being "too much in my head," in too big a hurry, worrying, judging, or trying to control things.

I use humor to lighten up.

When I lighten up, I make wiser choices and handle every situation with ease.

I release pent-up feelings and tensions when I laugh at myself as well as express my joy and happy feelings.

I lighten up with humor
and laughter.

Opening Communication

I open communication
with those people I care about.

I openly express myself about my feelings and
experiences when in conflict with another.

I let go of judgments and expectations and
accept what the other person expresses.

I listen "between the lines" to hear the real
messages the other person is sending, paying
attention to nonverbal cues, such as body
language and tone of voice.

When I do respond, I balance myself first, pay
attention to timing, limit critical and judgmental
words, and speak from my experience with
"I-messages."

I balance talking and listening.

---

*I open communication
with one person today.*

Relationship

I have or am attracting
the perfect partner for me.

I use my relationship as a way to learn about
myself, as my partner mirrors aspects of myself,
both positive and negative.

When I see traits in others that I dislike, I open
my mind to see that I may have these traits or
the potential for these traits.

If I want a relationship to be different, then
I have to be different.

If I want to transform or attract a relationship
that is more loving, giving, kind, forgiving,
authentic, and emotionally supportive, then I
have to be more loving, giving, kind, forgiving,
authentic, and emotionally supportive.

---

*I am learning to be the qualities I want to
experience in a primary love relationship.*

Clearing

I clear the clutter in my mind by allowing old memories to surface in order to neutralize their negative effects.

In meditation, I imagine lying on the shoreline at the edge of the beach and allowing the waves of memories and feelings to wash over me.

As the water subsides, I imagine hurtful memories and feelings leaving me and dissolving into the ocean.

I stand up with courage to face my future, allowing the new day to take root, grow, and blossom.

I clear out the old in order to bring in the new.

Self-Assurance

I am growing in self-assurance, trusting in
my healing process.

I am confident and comfortable with
who I am becoming.

As I trust the perfection of the awakening
process, I am self-assured to take more risks to
grow fuller into my potential Self.

I am self-assured as I successfully move forward
with each new step.

I see my confidence growing at
each stage of my growth.

*I am confident and self-assured as I allow
my true nature to unfold and blossom.*

Trust

I am a trusting person.

I no longer trust others more than I trust myself.

To take good care of myself, I listen to my inner knowing and body awareness in new situations.

I trust life is bringing me the perfect experiences to support my growth and healing.

I trust my intuition and awareness to guide and support me.

I trust each experience today to teach me more about myself and to expand my awareness.

Communion

I connect with and feel
part of the outdoors today.

I choose one aspect of nature to commune with:
a tree, a squirrel, a leaf, or a cloud.

I notice the colors, shapes, darks and lights,
and movement.

With my imagination I become one with
the Spirit within this aspect of nature and
experience its reality.

I enjoy this union and the exchange of energy
with this magnificent part of nature, both of us
giving and receiving.

---

*I enjoy feeling communion
with the Spirit in nature.*

Body Metaphors

My body speaks to me in metaphor.

I pay attention when I experience physical pain or illness, looking for clues telling me what is wrong and what I need.

I spend quiet time alone to crack the code of the metaphors of my body symptoms.

Sometimes I simply go with the pain and experience it to learn to overcome my fear.

I know my body is doing the best it can when it gets ill or is in pain, so I speak kindly to my body and nurture it.

I love and appreciate my body for being such a sensitive instrument registering my inner conflicts and giving me feedback through metaphor that something is out of balance in my life.

I crack the code of the metaphors my body uses to communicate its wisdom.

Weeding the Garden

I take inventory today of all the things I no longer want in the garden of my life.

Seeds planted in less aware days that are not in alignment with my present self are weeded and new ones are planted.

I look at my current surroundings and release items no longer valued or enjoyed, replacing them with things I love.

I pull the weed thoughts that stop my growth and plant new seed thoughts that support my goals, needs, and wants.

I weed the garden of my life, making room for the new to grow.

Cause and Effect

I pay attention to the law of cause and effect
operating in my life.

I understand that everything in my present
(effect) began as a thought and action
(cause) in my past.

I notice what I like in my life and look behind
this effect to see how I created this reality
so I can repeat it.

I take responsibility for my life by setting
new causes in motion today to create
new effects tomorrow.

I notice the positive consequences (effects)
of my new thoughts, feelings, words, and
visualizations (causes) and I like them.

---

*I am empowered to be the cause of good
effects in my life.*

Playing My Hand

I continue to expand my awareness in order to participate fully in the game of life.

I willingly play the hand I'm dealt each day to the best of my ability.

I watch myself as I go through all experiences — the challenging ones as well as those that uplift — remembering I have choices and lessons to learn.

I observe where I can make positive changes, letting more good into my life.

---

*I creatively play
the hand I'm dealt each day.*

Strengths

I celebrate my strengths, my positive traits,
and the things I do well.

I give up my old habit of only focusing on
what I see as my negative qualities.

I now recognize the importance of reminding
myself often of my good points and I take the
time today to list my positive traits
in my journal.

I also include ways to use the traits, behaviors,
and attributes that I judge as negative
in positive ways.

I am successful in all that I do because of my
strengths — my positive attitude, willingness
to take risks and learn from mistakes, and how
I live with high integrity. I am proud of my
strengths and how I give my life my best.

I feel the power of my strengths.

Summer Solstice

Summer is here and I enjoy this year's longest
day of greatest light, the summer solstice.

It's very symbolic in my life today as I shine the
light of understanding onto my path
to grow in awareness.

I align myself with the greater rhythm
of the earth.

I enjoy this time of greater activity,
growth, and progress.

---

*I align with the natural rhythm of life
today during the summer solstice.*

Joyful

I feel joy in this moment and in this day,
focusing in on my blessings.

I sometimes hurt in the growth process;
however, today I take a break and simply find
what is good and joyful.

I am joyful from the level of my soul knowing
that I have found the way.

I feel the fullness of my whole being.

*I feel joyful
today.*

Conflicts

I spend time alone when I have a conflict
with another to study the situation.

I no longer suppress or deny my feelings
during or after a confrontation.

I look behind conflicts to see what my part is
and where I have opportunities for growth.

I ask myself questions such as: "What is this
really about, what is going on below the surface?
What did I not see that caught me off guard?
What patterns am I healing? What would I like
to do differently?"

When appropriate I go back to the one I am in
conflict with to open communication, to find
ways to understand one another and resolve
our differences.

---

*I seek win-win solutions to resolve
conflicts with others.*

Dependency

I understand that it's normal to feel needy at
times and that as a child I may not have had my
dependency needs met at all times.

I pay attention to unrealistic dependency needs
that I expect others to fulfill, remembering that
this is unfair and an impossible task
for another to meet.

I nurture myself when I feel needy and do the
inner work necessary to heal and grow.

When feeling low because another cannot hold,
touch, or listen to me, I remember to go within
and seek nurturing for my inner child of the past
from my spiritual Self.

I enjoy healthy dependency when another
chooses to give, nurture, and care for me and
respond to my needs.

---

*I nurture my inner child when
dependency needs surface.*

Inner Work

Only I can change my life and I realize it requires
a commitment to do inner work.

I spend time alone each day to focus on the
inner work needed to improve my life.

I listen to my deeper feelings and thoughts,
allowing my unconscious to speak to me.

I walk outside, exercise, take a nap, or read
inspirational books that feed my longing for
wholeness and higher consciousness.

I write in my journal to process my feelings and
build awareness.

---

*I spend time daily doing
the inner work necessary to heal myself
and improve my life.*

Religious Guilt

I release guilt for choosing a new spiritual path
different from my early conditioning.

I give myself permission to question religious
teachings and explore new ideas.

I use my inner knowing to guide me in my desire
to know God personally in the way that suits me.

I respect religious traditions and look at the
symbolism behind the rituals and ceremonies to
find new meaning for me.

It's no longer important how I worship and
connect spiritually, it's only important that I do.

---

*I connect to God in my own way,
releasing religious guilt projected onto me
from well-meaning others.*

Family History

I look at my family history today to understand
the roots I have come from, looking at the
matrix of emotional patterns, beliefs, and values
that were passed on to me from
my family of origin.

I appreciate and accept the positive patterns and
choose to heal the negative patterns, moving
beyond any negative effects.

I acknowledge those who came before me
in my family lineage and know each is a
valuable part of me.

*I understand myself better by studying my
family history.*

Active Intelligence

I actively seek to build my intelligence.

I use my mind to evaluate choices and
help me make decisions.

I think before I speak or take action.

My mind, used at its best, steers my words
and actions.

My intelligence moves me to greater freedom,
awareness, and wholeness.

I spend time each evening pondering all that
happens in my day in order to make changes and
grow in understanding and awareness.

My intellect is my friend and it helps me make
wise choices.

---

*I use my active intelligence to seek
greater awareness and live with
right speech and right action.*

Comfort

I seek appropriate nurturing and comfort from
family and close friends.

I find comfort in spending time alone to
understand my needs, goals,
and my relationships.

I find comfort in accepting the kind ear of a
friend, love from a pet, or guidance from my
favorite book or teacher.

I receive comfort from people a step ahead of me
on the journey; they are my role models
as I continue to grow and evolve.

---

*I receive great comfort from others who
love and support me.*

Dislikes

Sometimes it's difficult to know what I want in life, so I pay attention to my dislikes.

I use this information to help me discover what I truly like and value.

I stop using my dislikes to complain, stay stuck, or to criticize myself or others, but rather to discover what I want to create for myself.

I take the time to think deeply when my dislikes surface.

I use my dislikes to help me see where I need to make changes in my life and what I want to create, experience, and enjoy in my future.

*I use my dislikes
to help me see what I like.*

Synchronicity

I look back at the series of coincidences
that have shaped my life.

I notice the synchronicity of events which at first
seemed to cross my path by chance, but in fact
turned out to be of great value and significance.

I see synchronistic events as part of the creative
process for my life as I unfold and
reach greater potential.

I anticipate new experiences "finding" me as I
grow in my awareness of the synchronicity of
"chance" encounters.

*I allow the synchronicity of events to
move my life in directions I might
never have considered.*

The Earth

I honor the earth and all she provides.

Mother Earth loves and supports me.

I feel gratitude for the great beauty of this planet.

I receive nourishment from the rainbow of colors in nature, the flowers, trees and foliage, water, and mountains.

I respect the earth, taking care to honor her resources and I do such things as recycle and not litter.

*I love the earth
and the earth loves me.*

Roadblocks

I make a list of roadblocks that keep me
stuck in old patterns.

I observe where I get in my own way, stopping
the growth process and the fun of living.

I spend time removing one roadblock today.

I first observe and analyze the situation to begin
figuring out the underlying dynamics.

I create affirmations and visualizations.

As I move forward in facing the roadblocks
in my life, I know I have the power to move
through them.

I take one positive risk today.

I honestly face the roadblocks on my path
and powerfully move forward
using my full awareness.

The Land of Opportunity

I celebrate living in this land of opportunity.

I am grateful to live in a country with a theme of equality, personal freedom, and opportunity.

I meet this responsibility with high integrity, monitoring my actions, thoughts, words, and feelings to respect my own and the freedoms of others.

I visualize every citizen of the world enjoying a life of creative opportunity and choice.

I am grateful to live in this land of opportunity which supports me growing into my Full-Potential Self.

Light

I create a home and body that is full of
light and radiance.

I shine the light of awareness in all the
dark corners of my life.

I lighten my diet, clear my physical space to
allow easy movement, clean my car, and spend
time improving my relationships.

I release old beliefs, habits, and patterns of living
in the dark and being unaware.

I share the light of awareness with others
who are interested.

I easily light the way for others who are in need.

---

*I build a lighted house within, a place of
refuge and comfort for myself and others.*

Soul

I watch as the negative influence of my
conditioned personality wanes and the authority
of my soul waxes.

I live from the place of spiritual purpose
and good will.

I begin or continue a daily spiritual practice,
a quiet time to connect and listen.

I allow my personality to be the perfect vessel
for the energy of my soul to manifest the
person I was created to be.

*I allow my soul to guide my life
with ease, joy, and glory.*

Freedom

I enjoy my new freedom.

I have found my way out of the labyrinth of illusion and being unaware.

I joyfully walk the path of enlightenment.

I leave behind the dead ends, pain and suffering, feeling like a victim, and the spinning of wheels that lead nowhere.

I grow daily, feeling more and more freedom, releasing myself from the hold of old limiting beliefs, habits, patterns, and interpretations of life.

I welcome the power of transformation in my life. I am free to discover more about my true nature and actualizing my potential.

---

*I enjoy the freedom
to be me.*

Secret

Wholeness is a secret, so I keep private
my inner healing and awakening.

I do not expect anyone to understand
or even notice my progress.

I practice silence when those close to me
do not understand or support my journey
into higher consciousness.

When I need to share my journey, I do so only
with those who show sincere interest or who are
also walking the path of self-discovery, inner
healing, and seeking greater Truth.

I respect where each person is in awareness and
do not burden others with information when
they are not yet ready to know the secrets of the
transformational journey.

---

*I am grateful to be on the journey to
wholeness and enjoy my secret.*

Negative Thoughts

I listen to the voice in my mind, paying special attention to the negative, critical words.

I change the negative self-talk to express the new truths I'm learning, such as seeing my inner beauty and feeling my innate worthiness.

I ask people who I trust to help me uncover more of my negative behaviors and thoughts so I can update them.

I stop being critical, negative, and judgmental toward myself and others.

Once I discover a negative thought, I turn it around into a positive, healthy affirmation.

I overcome negative thoughts by saying kind, loving, encouraging words to myself.

Loving Relationships

I experience loving relationships to the degree
that I love myself.

I begin this day by focusing my attention on
loving and accepting myself more.

I set an intention to be more loving
in my relationships.

I take the time to really listen to
the people I care about.

I send warm and loving thoughts to my partner,
children, parents, siblings, friends,
co-workers, and community.

---

*I build
loving relationships.*

Staying Present

I practice staying present and aware in all of today's unfolding experiences.

I concern myself only with what I need to do today.

If I can do something today to affect tomorrow, then I do it.

Otherwise, I stop worrying about tomorrow.

If I find myself reliving the past or daydreaming about the future, I bring myself back to the present moment.

When others are talking I give them my complete attention.

I focus on getting the most from today.

I allow my day to unfold,
staying present in each moment.

Power

I am powerful.

I feel my power growing as a self-aware,
loving, and creative person.

I use my power wisely for my own and
others' best interests.

I align myself with the Higher Power to live with
high integrity, right speech, and right action.

I accept my creative power
to actualize my potential.

It feels good to be a powerful co-creator
for good with God.

*I feel my power
and use it wisely.*

Tolerance

I practice tolerance throughout my day.

When people do not behave to my liking, I drop
my judgments and look behind their behavior
to see what is motivating them.

I have compassion for unaware ways people
communicate and behave.

I learn from them; they show me behaviors and
beliefs that I do not want to choose.

I notice my emotional reactions and remember
to practice love and forgiveness as
I build tolerance.

Understanding and tolerance does not mean I
accept abuse, so I confront or remove myself
from any situation attempting to harm or take
advantage of me.

---

*I practice tolerance of others and I set
appropriate boundaries for myself.*

Limitations

I look at boundaries, habits, roles, and guiding
beliefs that place limitations on my growth,
freedom, and creativity.

I explore each to see which have
any current validity.

I release outdated restrictions that limit me
in unhealthy ways.

I look for doorways of expansion and hidden
passageways out of my current limitations.

I walk through new thresholds and enter the
world of greater awareness and creative living.

I seek to expand my horizons.

---

*I release limitations and walk through
the doorway of my creative potential.*

Success

I accept every experience, both positive and
negative, as contributing to the
success of my life.

Unpleasant feeling experiences catch
my attention, showing me choices with
consequences that I do not want to repeat.

I enjoy success and meeting my goals.

It empowers me to know I can create
new outcomes.

I appreciate the progress I have made so far in
learning to love and accept myself, build better
relationships, and have a rich inner spiritual life.

*I know my life
is a success.*

Proud

When I stand face to face with myself, I am proud to be me.

I release old feelings and thoughts of being ashamed of who I am or for making poor, unaware choices in the past.

I focus on the lessons learned and remind myself of the power I now have to choose wisely.

I am proud of myself for all the time spent learning new ideas and getting to know my true Self.

I am proud of the changes in my behavior, my relationships, and the overall quality of my life.

I am proud
to be me.

Learning

I make a list of things I want to learn and do.

It does not matter how old I am or what my physical conditions are.

If I'm interested in developing a skill or experiencing something new or growing in a new direction, I put it on the list.

I begin planning and daydreaming about where to start taking risks.

I read my list often.

I visualize and feel the joy of learning new things.

Today is the perfect time to learn something new.

I love learning new things.

Roles

I take note of all the roles I play.

I evaluate how well these roles are supporting me and my relationships with others.

I ask myself questions such as: "Have I outgrown and want to change some of my roles or renegotiate others? Are any roles unhealthy to continue?"

I go within to plan how to change the roles that no longer serve me.

If these changes will affect people close to me, I begin talking to them about my desire to change, taking the time to listen and encourage them to consider making changes, too.

Some roles I choose to continue because it supports me and the higher functioning of the relationship or group.

***I play my roles with awareness
and with choice.***

Feeling Blue

I listen to my inner needs, fears, and conflicts
when feeling blue, depressed, or out of sorts.

I pay special attention to the ones I try to deny
or hide from myself.

I remember to do the things that anchor me
so I can heal and feel good again.

I look for ways to nurture myself: listening to
music, looking at flowers, sitting or walking
in nature, spending time with a close friend,
reading a cherished book, etc.

As I tune in to myself, I determine what needs
attention and the next step to take
to further heal.

---

*I tune in to myself when feeling blue to
understand what needs my attention.*

Subconscious Mind

My subconscious mind does not think and is
similar to a computer.

It manifests results based on my personal
interpretations of life; many of the beliefs,
perceptions, and images running the program are
not accurate or helpful.

Today, I am empowered by knowing I can
positively change any faulty programming.

I send new messages to my subconscious mind in
order to experience new results in my life.

I use the power of affirmations and visualizations
to plant new ideas and pictures
in the garden of my mind.

---

*I have the power to improve my life by
changing my subconscious mind.*

Grief

I allow myself to grieve when I experience loss
such as the death of a loved one or pet, a divorce,
a health challenge, growing older, losing a job,
moving, retiring, or unmet dreams and goals.

Grieving is part of my healing process.

I look back at my life and notice the things
that I need to release, forgive, and accept
in order to move on.

Completing the grieving process is a high
priority so I choose one experience to heal.

To help resolve my grief, I might need to feel my
angry or sad feelings, cry, or write in my journal.

Expressing myself is important, so I share my
grief with others who support my emotional
growth and well-being.

---

*I grieve the losses
in my life.*

The Path

I celebrate being on the path to higher
consciousness and wholeness.

Life is much easier now, as I easily recognize
those wiser than myself who can
show me the way.

I take responsibility for my life — to create,
to heal, to grow, and to give back.

Ahead of me on the path, I see light and
openness, which represents
my unrealized potential.

My future looks bright and I am excited
to step forward on my path.

---

*I celebrate
being on the Path.*

Time

Time is my friend.

I manage my time to include the things I want
to do, learn, explore, and experience.

When pressured with too many things to
accomplish, I have a serious talk with myself to
reset priorities and to determine
what can be released.

If I'm bored and spend too much time alone
or being passive, I also have a serious talk with
myself about being willing to take risks in order
to add more fun, companionship,
and activity in my life.

I balance my time wisely between
doing and being.

---

*I have time to do the things I must do,
as well as to play and have fun.*

Remembering

I remember who I am: a wonderful, growing, experiencing child of God.

I grow daily in remembering to express my true essence and be my true Self.

I feel connected to all of life and play the important game of being myself.

When I experience pain, fear, or anxiety, I soothe my "little self" by remembering the truth of who I really am.

My higher consciousness takes over when I remember my spiritual essence.

I experience deep peace and relaxation when remembering who I am.

Current Perspective

I like my current perspective on life.

I feel deep peace as I trust the light of my inner knowing to illuminate my path today.

As I turn around to review my life, I see the plan clearly and realize that it all makes sense from my current perspective.

The pain and suffering I endured helped me be a person today of great compassion and understanding.

I like my current perspective of being an aware, self-actualizing person.

I Am

"I am" are words of power and allow me to resonate with God or Higher Consciousness.

I appreciate the gift of my life and no longer take my life and creative power for granted.

I am an individualized spark of Life transforming daily, realizing my calling and my individual purpose.

I am co-creating with others for the good will of the world.

I play my part by living each day with awareness and allowing God to express through me.

***I am one with God
and all Life.***

Children

I love, appreciate, and enjoy children, my own children and grandchildren if I have them.

They help me remember the spark of spontaneity within me that is ready to meet with excitement and curiosity whatever comes my way.

I feel appreciation for the joy children bring.

I express interest, warmth, and gratitude to the children in my family or the first child I meet today.

I allow children to remind me of the open, innocent, and curious child I once was.

*I allow children
to brighten my day.*

Living Love

As I go through my day, I extend love to all
others, sometimes openly and
sometimes silently.

I let love in and allow others to love me.

I live with the intention to treat all people with
respect and loving kindness whether or not I
have an active relationship with each.

As I watch the world play out its dramas, I add
peace to the world by stopping my judgments
and simply loving others, many times
from a distance.

I stop concerning myself about what others are
or are not doing and continue living my life,
loving myself, and extending love to all others.

I quietly live each day being loving.

***I am empowered
by living love.***

Recovery

I appreciate the process of recovery
operating in my life.

I realize it takes time to heal and recover from
the wounds of the past, to change negative
thinking patterns, as it does to end addictions to
substances, people, or to things having
to be a certain way.

I go easy on myself when I push too hard to
make changes and they do not stick.

I accept the process of inner healing and do the
inner work necessary to get past my blocks and
to create the results I want.

I am humble when I find others a step ahead of
me on the path and let them nurture me and
show me the way. I turn and help others who
need my assistance.

---

*I take one step today on my healing
journey of recovering.*

Self-Acceptance

I love and accept myself.

I grow daily in understanding and accepting
the suppressed and unhealed parts of me that
surface and surprise me at times.

I am understanding and integrating all parts of
myself — those I like, as well as those I dislike.

I am a whole person now that I accept
all aspects of myself.

Self-acceptance grows as I shine the light of
understanding on myself.

---

*I fully accept myself
as I am, today.*

Teachers

I listen to my inner guidance and gut level feelings when considering a new teaching or following a teacher.

I pay close attention to how information resonates within me before I follow the teachings of a teacher, author, TV personality, minister, priest, rabbi, or guru.

I pay attention to my intellect, my body awareness, and my inner knowing to determine whether or not a teacher is right for me.

When I feel lightness and a deep peace, I move toward a teacher or teaching and move away when I feel heaviness or darkness.

A mentor or teacher is right for me when I feel more connected to my true Self.

I easily recognize and attract teachers who resonate with me and help me progress on my journey.

Heart

Today, I open my heart to feel all
the goodness in my life.

I am the gatekeeper to my heart and can open
and close the gate at will.

I open my heart to experiences that feel right
and move me in a healthy direction.

When situations are challenging, I stay open and
aware, asking myself questions like: "How can
I see this through the eyes of love? What am I
learning? What new responses do I now have?
What is the most loving thing
I can do at this time?"

I appreciate all the good things happening in my
life and continue to open to new
situations and people.

---

*I open my heart and feel the
goodness in my life.*

Physical Appearance

I love and accept my physical body.

I am at peace with the things I do not like about my physical form that can't be changed.

If I'm dissatisfied with an aspect of my appearance that I have control over, such as my weight, I set a realistic plan to make a positive change.

I work well with my appearance, choosing clothing and hair styles that become me.

I allow beauty from my inner presence to radiate outward, thus enhancing my physical appearance.

My thoughts affect my appearance, so I maintain a positive mental attitude. I smile and laugh a lot, which positively affects my looks.

---

*I accept my
physical appearance.*

Food

Food is my friend and I thank the food I eat for nourishing and rebuilding my body.

I easily choose a wholesome diet including a reasonable amount of comfort foods.

I avoid extreme eating patterns, such as over-eating, deprivation of food, or fad diets.

I listen to my body's cues that let me know when I'm hungry and when I'm full.

I forgive myself for the times I do not listen, simply vowing to begin anew eating foods that serve me.

I bless the food that I eat and let my body process it for my highest good.

I enjoy eating and I nourish my body with wholesome food.

New Life

I feel joyful as I watch my new life unfolding.

It excites me living with the daily discoveries of my true, authentic Self.

I am happy about my new awareness and am cracking the code of negative patterns and challenges in order to bring in new growth with new possibilities.

I am excited to continue my journey, discovering new ways to live in the world and not getting caught in the illusions of old patterns.

---

*I am excited about
my new life unfolding.*

Compassion

I feel deeply when others are hurting.

I show compassion when others struggle.

My friends know they can talk to me because I
easily empathize when each feels pain
or suffers emotionally.

I have compassion for all the people in the world
struggling to find their way and I say a silent,
healing prayer for them all.

When undergoing a life challenge and in need
of support and understanding, I appreciate and
accept the compassion of my friends.

I have kind thoughts, words, and actions for all
the people I meet in my life today.

*I am a
compassionate person.*

Animals

I pay attention to and appreciate animals,
as they enrich my life.

I receive love and companionship
from a beloved pet.

I learn a lot about myself by watching animals
interact, play, and meet their needs.

I observe an animal in nature today,
like a bird, squirrel, or rabbit.

I communicate, with words or telepathically,
with this animal and experience
the oneness between us.

It comforts me to spend time with
an animal today.

---

*I appreciate the gifts
of the animal kingdom.*

Connectedness

I feel connected to my true Self as I align my body, mind, and spirit.

The connectedness I feel within myself and to other people helps me easily manage any drama that may surface in my day.

I concentrate on what is really important and see the larger scheme of things, noticing patterns, themes, and lessons.

I focus on feelings of connectedness and on being a part of all Life.

I feel whole and complete right now as I allow my true Self to shine.

I feel connected
to my true Self.

Plants

I love and appreciate the beauty that plants
bring to the world.

I enjoy the colors and smells
of the plant kingdom.

I allow plants, flowers, and trees to nurture and
soothe me when I'm stressed.

A walk in a park or a garden calms
and balances me.

I practice extending my mind to commune with
a plant, flower, or tree in order
to feel our oneness.

---

*I spend time with plants, trees, and
flowers to balance my emotions and feel
their healing energy.*

Sunlight

My life depends on the life-sustaining
energy of the sun.

I enjoy sunlight and gladly receive energy
from the sun today.

I spend a few minutes in sunlight to experience
the full spectrum of light, which is necessary
for my health.

I appreciate the process of photosynthesis, which
allows me to consume the energy of the sun in
the form of the plants I eat and to breathe in the
energy of the sun from the air.

I live in gratitude for the light
the sun shines on me.

---

*I enjoy
sunlight.*

Inner Balance

I live my life with inner balance, avoiding extremes in thoughts, words, or actions.

I pay attention to any part of me that is out of sync, so I can do positive things to get back in alignment.

I focus on one thing today that is out of balance in myself and make a correction; maybe I have spent too much time recently on achievement and reaching my goals at the expense of an important relationship.

I notice the things that support my inner balance and commit to making them a daily habit.

*I maintain my
inner balance today.*

Deep Peace

I allow deep peace to flow into my life.

As I learn to practice continual love and forgiveness, I enjoy deep inner peace — which I then extend to my outer world.

Peaceful thoughts and words repeated often to myself dissolve my conflicts.

Each person I meet or pass today, I silently greet them by affirming, "Peace be with you."

May each, at least for a moment, feel calm and peaceful because of my presence.

Deep peace prevails in my life.

I feel deep peace within me and reflect it to all others.

Color

I enjoy all the colors of the rainbow.

I use color in my environment and clothing to positively influence my emotional well-being.

I notice the colors that balance me and help me feel good.

If, for example, I feel scattered and am moving too quickly, I may choose to wear cool, calming colors of blue, green, or violet to help slow me down and balance me.

If I need energy, I may simply visualize and breathe in a warm color such as red or orange, or I might look at a red flower, a colorful painting, or stand in the sunshine for a few minutes.

I am the artist of my day, painting with a full palette of colors.

Nurturing Others

I like to nurture others.

Giving is easy for me and I take notice
where my energy is truly needed.

I recognize the difference between people who
benefit from my nurturing and those
who continually take and refuse to learn to
nurture themselves.

Those who need to learn self-nurturing benefit
from my encouragement and not from my doing
too much for them.

I teach self-nurturing by modeling it and
not by creating dependency.

*I am a
nurturing person.*

Assignment

I have a special assignment and purpose.

I start by accepting the assignment
to be uniquely me.

I love and accept myself right now, this moment.

I choose to become more aware of the reasons
why I am here, so I can actualize
my spiritual purpose(s).

I pay attention to my interests and my talents,
as they are part of my assignment, to be
developed and used.

My purpose unfolds as I grow in awareness.

---

*I accept the assignment to be uniquely
me, creatively expressing my interests and
talents for the good of all.*

Reawakening

I am reawakening to who I already am.

I knew at birth that I was a spiritual being having the experience of a human being.

I no longer allow the early conditioning of my childhood to hold me back from the awareness of my true nature.

I express more each day of my innate goodness.

I accept the human part of me that learned randomly, at first, through a lot of pain, struggle, and unhappiness.

This process of pain and suffering now quickens my reawakening through the light of understanding and awareness. I accept my spiritual heritage and release all feelings of unworthiness.

I reawaken to the awareness that
I am a spiritual being having
a human experience.

Vessel

My body is a vessel for Spirit.

It's my privilege to be a channel for the love and light of Spirit to use my talents and gifts in service for the good will of others.

It's a great opportunity to be alive in this dynamic period in time and to know that I am a living expression of God.

I thank each cell in my body for living its purpose in order to give me a physical vehicle to be used as a perfect vessel for Spirit.

I am a perfect vessel for Spirit to use in service to humanity.

Deepening Relationships

I understand the importance of building a deeper foundation of trust, understanding, and caring in my close relationships.

When in conflict with a close friend or family member, I choose to drop the old script that makes any other person the "bad guy."

I realize we are all doing our best with our level of understanding and awareness, so choose to communicate and understand the other person.

I choose to see the good qualities in others and practice tolerance and forgiveness.

I take a risk with one person today to deepen feelings of closeness and intimacy.

I set a goal to deepen my relationship with all the people I care about.

I have the power to deepen
my relationships.

Looking Within

I look within to find my true nourishment.

My spiritual essence reveals itself as I learn to go within and do my spiritual practices such as meditation, contemplation, affirmative prayer, and journal writing.

As I practice self-inquiry, I question my motivations for acting in certain ways, building awareness and integrity with myself.

I am learning to tell the difference between my conditioned personality self and my true Self.

It feels good to get to know and express my true nature.

*I look within
as my true Self reveals itself.*

Relating with Feeling

My conflicts with others dissipate as I relate on a feeling level.

I sense the feelings behind others' words.

I notice body language — mine and theirs.

My power of relating increases as I slow my reactions and I stop telling, advising, or trying to change or fix others.

Instead, I allow others to drink from the oasis of my cool, clear, refreshing water of unconditional love and greater awareness as I relate on a feeling level.

I accept what others have to say and what they are feeling, even if it's not to my liking. I understand that acceptance and listening do not require agreement.

I improve communication by relating on a feeling level with others.

Perceptions

I perceive life through new eyes.

I do not perceive old issues or challenges as something to be ashamed of, but simply as lessons to be learned and resolved.

I see the value in releasing worry, fear, and judgment.

I concern myself with living in the present moment to solve my problems and I do not look too far into the future or keep rehashing the past.

I perceive the perfection of all my experiences and integrate them into my conscious awareness.

I perceive my life experiences through new eyes.

Adventure

I see my life as an adventure as I explore
uncharted territory, taking positive risks.

Today, I choose an area to explore that is
outside of my comfort zone.

I may choose something on the physical level
such as walking outside alone, singing, or
signing up for a yoga class.

I may explore emotionally by joining a support
or study group, taking a class or seminar, or
begin journal writing for self-discovery.

I can grow mentally by reading a book outside
my usual area of interest or belief system or by
practicing new communication skills
with my family.

I can take a spiritual risk by creating a sacred
space to begin meditating daily.

*I see my life as an adventure with
continuous, exciting, new things to explore.*

Spontaneity

I listen to my inner playful self today
and live with spontaneity.

Rather than get bogged down with my lessons,
daily structure, self-discipline and responsibility,
I choose to lighten up, be more spontaneous, and
enjoy the side-trips as my day detours.

I appreciate those spontaneous moments that
allow me to exchange a smile with a stranger,
a janitor, or a child.

These brief connections of the heart are felt
everywhere I go today.

I lighten up and
live with spontaneity.

Anger

I acknowledge all my feelings,
including my anger.

I feel my anger when it surfaces and use its
energy to make positive changes.

I stop fearing other people's anger and
allow each their own experiences.

If I feel scared and begin to take responsibility
for another's anger, I stop, detach, and remove
myself from the scene if it's directed at me.

I remember that angry people project onto
others when they feel powerless and fearful
and do not take responsibility for their own
emotional health.

I acknowledge my own anger and process it
without blaming or hurting others.

---

*I take responsibility for feeling only my
own anger and use it wisely to make
positive changes in my life.*

Enlightenment

I move forward with greater realizations today.

I am in the process of "lightening" my life, letting go of old patterns of thinking, speaking, and acting as I develop greater awareness.

I walk through doorways drawing me forward, enabling me to grow in understanding.

I enjoy the degree of enlightenment I experience right now and see it continuing.

I trust the enlightenment process unfolding in my life to always take me to the next place I need for my awakening.

I share with others a step behind me on the path the light that I now possess.

I expand my awareness daily on the journey of enlightenment.

My Rights

I have the right to be heard and to express my point of view with friends and family.

I have the right to say no as well as yes.

I take care of myself when another oversteps my boundaries, by opening communication or leaving the situation if abusive.

I take risks to bring up issues that bother me with my close friends or with individuals in my family.

I assert myself without being aggressive.

I work through my own feelings in order to do a good job communicating with others.

I pay attention to my rights as well as the rights of others, communicating openly and honestly.

Loving Myself

I concentrate on loving myself today.

My self-esteem grows daily.

I no longer turn this job over to others, realizing people can only love me to the degree they love themselves.

I do enjoy it when another can listen to me and give me love, attention, and support.

I catch myself when I become overly needy or dependent on another and get myself back on track by being responsible for my own well-being.

I remember, at these times, to set aside quality alone time to do my healing practices: prayer, meditation, saying affirmations, or sitting quietly in nature in order to return to the place of deep inner peace.

I feel warm and loving
toward myself.

Critical Mass

I am more self-aware now and less stuck
in old thinking patterns and behavior.

The inner battle between the old and the
new is quieting, as the critical mass of higher
consciousness rules.

My life is much easier now, as I view my issues,
problems, and conflicts as merely things I
undergo in order to heal and grow.

I watch the majority of myself living in
the light as I march to the beat and
rhythm of my true Self.

I know I am an important part of the critical
mass of the planet, adding my weight to
manifesting peace and respect for all
individuals' rights and interests.

*I accept the critical mass changing my
life from darkness into light.*

Wholeness

I am a whole and complete human being.

I am enough by myself.

I do not need other people to complete me or to make me a whole person.

I continue to do my inner work and to love myself completely.

As I spend quiet time alone filling myself with healing energy from Spirit and love from the God within, I realize my wholeness.

I joyfully meet my experiences today, because my security comes from within and not from a dependency on others or outer events.

I interact with others from my place of wholeness, uplifting all I meet.

I am whole and complete right now.

Control

I understand the only person whom I have
control over is myself.

I take full responsibility for controlling myself
— my thoughts, actions, emotions,
choices, attitudes.

I observe myself when wanting to control
situations and people to discover my own issues:
not feeling safe, understood, respected, or heard.

Control of others lessens and compassion grows
as I focus on my own life, healing my issues,
knowing and loving myself, and living creatively
to actualize my talents, interests, and purposes.

I feel freedom and deep peace
as I simply allow.

---

*I let go of control,
and flow.*

Spiritual Power

I have the power to create my life the way I want.

The source of my power is my spiritual
connection to God or All That Is.

I align with my Spiritual Self to receive creative
solutions to my challenges and to see the many
possibilities to actualize my potential.

I clear my mind to receive ideas and impressions
about what to create, many times empowering
others, not just myself.

I visualize and affirm these impressions and
ideas, and I allow others to help me bring
them to fruition.

I have gratitude
in accepting my real power.

---

*I allow my spiritual power to co-create
the highest good for myself and others.*

*My Father**

I honor the man who is or was my father in life.

He played an important role for my life script.

I send him love and peace to help him grow
further on his journey.

I release any residue of anger or hurt for unmet
expectations or needs.

I forgive my dad for what he could not give.

I accept that he played his part in my script to
the best of his abilities. I internalize the positive
things I received from my father.

My inner father loves and protects me.

** This passage may be read on
your own father's birthday.*

---

*I am grateful for all I received
from my father.*

Garden

My life is like a garden and I am the gardener.

I nurture the garden of my mind continually,
pulling the weed thoughts of limited thinking
and planting new seed thoughts of love,
fulfillment, and well-being.

I fertilize my garden with affirmations and
visualizations of abundance.

I allow energy from nature and the help of kind
friends and wise teachers to boost
my gardening skills.

*I tend the garden of my life
with great care.*

Maintenance

I give attention to what it takes to
maintain my physical world.

I do at least one thing each day to take care of
my material possessions.

I take inventory of the things in my home that
need to be fixed, replaced, washed, painted,
or thrown away.

I make a realistic maintenance plan.

I do the same for maintaining my physical body,
noting if I need more rest, activity, higher quality
food, an eye exam, etc.

My life is easier when I address the necessity
of maintaining my physical possessions, home,
yard, car, and body. A little maintenance every
day lightens my load.

---

*I value a little maintenance a day to keep
my life ordered and simple.*

Criticism

I stop my internal critic by focusing
on my positive traits.

I detach from the criticism and
judgments of others.

I no longer need an outside authority to approve
of me or direct my life.

I make my own decisions based on my current
awareness and spiritual guidance, so I drop the
criticism when results are less than
perfect at times.

I have an overall positive sense of my own
well-being as I mature in awareness.

---

*I let go of internal and external criticism,
focusing on making the best of
my decisions.*

Spiritual Practice

I focus in on the spiritual practices
that I know improve my life.

I recommit to a morning or evening devotional
time to read and study spiritual material.

I nurture my soul with meditation
and prayer daily.

I choose a religious teacher or spiritual person
on whom to pattern my life.

I progress on my journey to higher
consciousness by maintaining my
spiritual practices.

*I commit to my
daily spiritual practice.*

Exercise

I like to maximize my physical strength and
health with regular exercise.

I take care of my physical body with exercise
designed for my needs, such as yoga, walking,
biking, Pilates, or playing a sport.

I walk often and use stairs whenever possible in
order to activate my physical energy level.

If my body is challenged, I listen to my inner self
as I create a special program to meet my needs.

I create a strong physical form by
getting exercise daily.

*I give myself the gift
of regular, fun exercise.*

Acceptance

I joyfully love and accept myself now.

I go forth with an attitude of acceptance toward
myself and all others, monitoring
my critical mind.

I remind myself that each of us is doing the best
we can with our present awareness, so I choose
to continue expanding my awareness.

Acceptance does not mean I have to be around
someone who hurts me because
they are unaware.

I accept my new thoughts as they are improving
the quality of my life.

*I have genuine acceptance for everyone
I meet today.*

*Birthday**

Today is my special day.

I joyfully celebrate my birthday and being
another year wiser.

I thank my parents for providing this
opportunity to live my life.

As I look in the mirror, I say kind things to
myself like: "I love you. I'm taking good care of
you today and everyday. I am so happy
to be alive."

I celebrate my day and am not dependent on
others to make me happy or to even remember
it's my birthday.

I treat myself to self-nurturing as I celebrate my
innate worth and beauty.

*Exchange this passage with your birthday.

---

*I joyfully celebrate
my birthday today.*

Traits

I accept all my characteristics and traits.

I see my traits as neutral; they become positive
or negative depending upon how I use them.

I remind myself when unhappy with one of my
traits that each can also be expressed
in a positive way.

For example, a trait of being strong-willed can
get me into trouble in relationships at times;
however, it's also the trait I use to stay on the
transformational journey and to not give up
in changing my life.

It's always up to me and I choose to observe
myself continuously to positively
express my traits.

---

*I accept my unique set of personality
traits and express them positively.*

Friends

I care about my friends.

I appreciate the unconditional love and emotional support of my close friends.

I express gratitude to those who have shared my pain, sadness, joy, excitement, and breakthroughs.

I send love to all the people who have shared a part of my life with me.

I appreciate my friends and send them each a special blessing today and always.

Catalyst

I appreciate the people who have catalyzed my life and helped me move in new directions.

As I heal myself I am a catalyst for others.

I know when to be a catalyst in igniting the desire for awareness in another and when to let go, as each person must do the inner work to heal themselves.

I allow others to be dependent on me for a while as I watch the kindled fire within each begin to blaze on its own.

True nurturing comes from helping others to discover their own ability to maintain the inner fire of desire for change.

I'm a catalyst, encouraging others to do what I have learned to do for myself.

I am a catalyst for other people's growth and healing.

Important

My life is important and counts in more ways
than I can understand.

Even if it feels that I'm blindly stumbling along
at times, I know in my heart that I am a part of
Life's special plan.

I know now to let go and trust my process, even
if things do not always make sense
to my logical mind.

Sometimes I understand on an intellectual level,
but it's usually at a feeling level that I know the
importance of my life.

I gain comfort in knowing I make a difference
to the world by just healing my own life and
learning to be me.

---

*I know my life is important and I make a
difference in my own unique way.*

Pause

I enjoy the pauses after a period of being on the fast track of accelerated change.

I accept the times that seem slow with no obvious progress being made, as I need to balance out with rest periods.

When I feel stuck, I remind myself that I need a pause to digest all the new ideas and assimilate the changes.

I accept that I am in the perfect place on my life path at all times to learn and grow.

I remember to stay present and to look for and celebrate the joys of the moment during the pauses life gives me.

I enjoy a pause today from the fast pace of growing and changing.

Inner Guidance

I spend time daily tuning in to my inner guidance because this is a way of life for me now.

To solve my problems, heal pain, fear, and doubt requires that I listen to my inner knowing.

My path becomes clear as I trust my inner guidance system, which communicates with me in various ways: a hunch or gut level feeling, an image or vision, a still-quiet voice within, a passage from a book that speaks to me, or words a wise friend shares with me.

Each day I trust more and more my inner guidance to direct my life.

I use my inner guidance
to show me the way.

Integrating

At times, I feel as if I have different people
living inside me.

Some parts of me do not cooperate and are
child-like and immature, while other parts are
wise and resourceful.

I allow my wise self to nurture and guide
the wounded parts of me, as I grow into an
integrated, fully functioning, mature person.

I no longer suppress or deny the parts of me
I do not like.

I listen to my fearful, resistant parts.

I speak to myself with kind, supportive, yet
firm self-talk when I need cooperation to move
forward, much like a loving parent
talks to a child.

---

*I am integrating all parts of myself to
recognize my wholeness.*

Positive Intention

I understand now that each resistant, immature aspect of my personality has a positive intention, which was appropriate at certain times in my life.

As I discover the positive intention, which many times was to help me feel safe and to protect me, I thank that part of me for the job it has been doing.

Then, I reassure that part that I am more aware now and want to grow in a more fulfilling direction.

In order to transform the limiting parts of myself, I spend quality alone time to ponder, meditate, pray, or journal to help me process the information.

I listen to the positive intentions of resistant parts of myself as I transform and grow into a healthy, mature adult.

Greater Meaning

I have a choice in how I experience my day.

I am learning to live with greater meaning and awareness and moving beyond limited thinking.

I look for greater meaning especially while experiencing difficult people or situations.

I learn from all experiences and people and stop judging them as good or bad.

I open my mind and look behind issues, situations, dramas, and problems to make sense of them and to understand why I have drawn them into my life.

I accept that my life has greater meaning than I can understand at times.

I accept that everything happens for a reason so I look for greater meaning behind situations.

Co-Creating

I am connected to all other people in this experience of life, and thus share in the co-creation of outcomes.

I understand that the only control I have is over myself and my individual life.

When in a relationship, I remind myself that each brings a point of view.

I allow the time it takes to communicate as we learn to blend, compromise, and harmonize as we co-create our reality.

I forgive the unawareness of those who dominate larger groups, such as in the political arena, who make unwise choices. I know how important it is to play my part with high integrity, awareness, and wisdom.

I do my part in co-creating the best outcomes in my relationships and the collective group experience.

Quality of Life

I continue seeking to improve the quality of my life by healing myself and my relationships, building greater awareness, and looking for meaning in all I do.

I take responsibility for my own life and choose to focus on the things that bring improvement, satisfaction, and enjoyment.

The quality of my journey is up to me and me alone.

I no longer get distracted by pain, fear, and drama for long, because I remember to stay centered and present in all my experiences, drawing on my wisdom.

I discover joy and lightheartedness as I focus on the quality of life I live.

I take responsibility for continuously improving the quality of my life.

Pathways

New pathways are operating in my life.

To change, I must recognize places in my life where I'm stuck repeating negative patterns.

I begin building a new pathway by first admitting I have a problem.

I then consider my choices in order to break out of an old pattern, and then I take one step at a time to build a new pattern.

I focus on the new pathways working in my life so I can maintain them.

I remember to take the quiet time necessary to figure out the patterns in my life that I want to keep and those that need to change.

I have the power to change what I do not like in my life into new, positive, productive, enjoyable pathways.

Improvement

My life improves daily.

I see things differently now and celebrate
that I can make new, wiser choices.

I notice the little things that are improving, such
as accepting myself the way I am and not trying
to be anyone else.

I am optimistic about my future as I continue the
journey of self-improvement and living my life
to the fullest.

I am peaceful and relaxed as my life unfolds into
new levels of awareness and experience.

*I celebrate the improvements
in my life.*

Autumn Equinox

I celebrate this time of harvest as the seeds planted in the spring and nourished with the summer growing season come to fruition.

I align my own life with this rhythm.

Much has grown to fruition in my life.

The seed thoughts of higher truths are operating in my life now.

My awareness continues to grow, yet I feel comfortable with my current degree of awareness.

I understand so much about myself and my life now.

I experience deep peace much of the time no matter what is happening in my outer world.

I celebrate the autumn equinox as it symbolizes the harvest of my garden.

Double Agent

I am like a double agent, living my inner life from new perspectives.

I quietly live my daily life and know at the same time that I am tuned in to my inner, true Self.

I live with expanded awareness, willingly meeting my challenges and joys in order to continue healing the past, learning lessons, and creating a joyful life.

I have a special assignment to be my true Self and model my spiritual values quietly to others.

*I am a double agent
for Spirit.*

People

I accept that everyone is in my life for a reason.

Each person I have attracted is like a mirror, reflecting something about me that helps me experience more of myself.

These mirrors show me my positive side, as well as show me where I might choose to transform my personality.

I am open and observant to catch the subtle meaning in all my interactions with each person in my day.

I appreciate the people in my life who care about me, love me, and show an interest in me.

I dance with the people in my life to learn and grow from all my interactions with each of them.

Life as a Process

I see my life as a process, not as a goal
with a finish line.

I create my life paying attention to the
experiences moment to moment.

I stay open to all situations and experiences as I
go through my day knowing they are all part of
my life process.

I welcome the unexpected and see the detours
that take me off my intended course as
opportunities to learn and grow.

Sometimes the rerouting gives me possibilities
for greater growth than might have
been otherwise.

---

*I love my life as it unfolds in a
continuous process.*

Needs and Wants

I go within to observe and assess my needs in five areas of myself: physical, social, emotional, mental, and spiritual.

I release the blocks preventing me from determining my needs.

I am an adult now and it's okay to express what I need and want.

I'm no longer dependent upon others to meet my true needs.

In my journal, I list all the needs I'm conscious of right now in order to begin the process of meeting these needs.

I am worthy of recognizing and getting my real needs met and deserve to have the things I want.

I go within to discover my true needs and wants so I can nurture myself.

Service

I dedicate my life to serving others, now that I have examined my life and have experienced a lot of positive changes.

I have a good understanding of myself and how to care for myself.

I give of my talents and time to making this world a better place.

I do not get hooked into giving to every person and cause that crosses my path.

I discriminate between those people and situations that are a good match and complement my need to give and those that are not.

I have the ability to say "No," as well as, "Yes," to people, situations, and causes that need my help.

I choose
a life of service.

Wounds

I continue to heal the wounds from my past,
caused both from myself and others.

I no longer blame others who were unable to
love and nurture me, as they also were wounded.

I acknowledge myself for all that it took to get
here today and all the commitment it will take to
continue healing and growing.

I am joyful for my new awareness, which is
creating a better, more fulfilling life.

I focus today on the good things I now
experience, like being in control of
my own life now.

*I move forward continuing to heal the
wounds from my past.*

Now

It's always right now.

I focus my attention on this present moment.

Deep peace fills me as I let go of the past and any fear of the future and simply remain in the experience of now, today.

Right now is all there is, so I focus my attention on what I'm doing and what is happening to me today.

If there is something I need to handle to prepare for tomorrow I do it, without losing sight of what I need to do today.

I remain mindful of the events happening now.

I live in the now and relax into being fully present in all my experiences.

Money

I look at my relationship with money.

Does it slip through my fingers too easily or do I have a readily available supply? Do I spend more than I make or do I save for the future?

Do I only have enough money to cover my basic needs or do I have money to do the things I value beyond the basics?

I write down my beliefs about money; and wherever I find a negative charge, I begin identifying where it stops my flow.

I question beliefs that have a negative spin, by asking myself: "Where did I learn this? Is it true for everyone? Am I patterning myself after anyone else? How can I view things differently? What do I now believe is true?"

Money is my friend.

I enjoy having money.

Naive

I'm no longer naive in new situations.

I look behind first impressions because things are not always as they seem.

Rather than assume anything about anyone or anything too fast, I allow my curiosity to go exploring.

I use my power of observation and pay attention to things that feel "off."

I see that outer appearances are only the tip of the iceberg.

I take care of myself
and am no longer naive.

Polarities

I notice polarities in life and within myself.

I see the paradox in that opposites are really
different ends of the same continuum.

I know my joy because I have been depressed,
my positive attitude because I have been
negative, my happiness because I have been sad,
and my achievements because I have been bored,
stuck in a rut, and not willing to take a risk.

I see opposing parts of my personality, such as
my risk-taking side and my play-it-safe side; I
learn to use both sides at appropriate times.

I balance some polarities within myself by
learning moderation and blending.

*I allow the dance of polarities in my life
to be complementary.*

Tension

When I have a clash of wills with another or within different parts of myself, I do healthy things to balance myself and release tension.

I cry, exercise, clean house, step outside and deep breathe, make sounds (sighing, groaning, humming, etc.), clarify my thoughts with journal writing, or talk to a trusted friend.

I experience the release of tension similar to the calm after a thunderstorm.

After I release tension, I regain my inner peace and am ready to move forward.

I clear emotional tension when it arises so I can begin anew.

Stress

I check in with myself regularly to note my stress level, noticing if my muscles are tense, I am breathing too rapidly or am overly reactive to others or current situations.

When I feel out of step with myself, I regain my inner balance by taking slow, deep breaths.

I calm myself further by taking a moment to center myself, visualizing a cool, peaceful color, such as green or blue surrounding me or by simply looking at the sky.

I know life is a continual experience of ups and downs, so I have realistic expectations as I manage my level of stress.

*I practice calming techniques
to balance my stress level.*

Daily Purpose

I begin my day by asking to be of service.

I watch with expectancy for today's
special assignment.

I accept the detours that bring unexpected
meetings and situations with others.

Whatever presents itself I know I will learn
something of value and see where I am needed.

My purpose each day ranges from significant to
mundane, which I accept.

Step by step, I walk the path that is my life,
finding meaning and purpose each day.

---

*I watch with expectancy for
today's special purpose.*

Enthusiasm

I am enthusiastic about my life and that I have
the opportunity to make my own choices to
direct my day.

I play with the experiences that come
my way today.

I add enthusiasm to my personality to help me
sustain a positive mental attitude.

I allow enthusiasm to flow into my day's agenda.

I have a positive effect on others with my spirit
of enthusiasm.

*I am enthusiastic
about my life.*

Allowing

Once I do the inner work to clear away the old
and focus on creating the new, I must learn to let
go and allow.

Allowing means I have to accept the process and
proper timing before my wishes
come to fruition.

I understand that I cannot push the river to
move faster or dig up a seed to see
if it's sprouting.

Rather, I must let go and allow life its process
and develop patience.

I see that I'm not totally in control as I am
co-creating with other people and with God.

---

*I let go and let God, allowing results to
manifest in their proper time.*

Spiritual Heritage

I am a unique and incredible being; a human being with a spiritual essence.

I remember this when I get sidetracked by my issues and dramas.

I am an extension of the Source living in the physical world, much like a ray of sunshine streaming from the sun.

I quiet my mind chatter to feel the deep peace of my spiritual roots.

My self-esteem grows as I connect to my spiritual heritage.

I appreciate my spiritual heritage and feel that spark of life within me.

Transitions

I accept that I'm in an ever-changing world.

My life is exciting as change continually brings me new transitions.

I allow any fear, doubt, or insecurities to arise so I can manage any resistance to the new.

I remember to tell myself things like: "This is just an experience. You are strong now and perfectly capable to go forward. It takes time to adjust to new situations so take your time."

I look at all the new opportunities on the horizon to explore during the transition periods of my life.

Change is my friend and I go with the flow, letting go of resistance.

I accept the richness of new experience in each transition.

Restructuring

I am restructuring the foundation of my
thinking patterns and belief system.

I listen to my negative self-talk, as it gives me
clues to my faulty thinking.

I rewrite limiting thoughts and beliefs by
changing each negative/false comment into a
positive/true one.

I write my new thoughts in a journal
or on 3x5 cards to review often and to
read aloud to myself.

I read these new beliefs until I feel their truth
positively guiding my life.

Whenever I begin to hear negative comments
from my self-talk, I hear the new thoughts
override them.

---

*I am restructuring
the foundation of my life.*

Inner Child

I have the power to change the negative effects from my past.

I reconnect with my inner child of the past, communicating as a loving parent would.

I use words of encouragement to help the shut-down parts of myself open up and become part of my adult self.

Each day, I tune in to my inner child to help her/him express needs and wants.

If, for example, my inner child is feeling abandoned or lonely, I may sit in a rocking chair, listen to inspiring music, and imagine myself as a young child being rocked and comforted.

I love my inner child.

I nurture my inner child today in order to return to living openly, joyfully, and spontaneously.

Offensive Behavior

I practice tolerance when around people who think or behave in offensive, unkind, and unaware ways.

I practice forgiving them for offensive behavior and continue to love them at the impersonal level of mind (this is unconditional love that the Greeks call agape love).

I set clear boundaries and remove myself from situations if someone tries to use me as a scapegoat or target for their anger.

I take care of myself when in challenging situations around difficult people.

I practice tolerance, forgiveness, and agape love when around people with offensive behavior or thinking patterns.

Organic

My life is organic, alive, always
moving and growing.

I am comfortable now in allowing my life
to flow and change.

I grow with ease, pulling the roots of resistance.

I open to receiving the harvest of my gardening
skills, allowing good things to come my way.

My relationships are organic, too, growing and
transforming into rich, meaningful partnerships.

I have the strength of character to meet all that
life brings me.

*I see my life as organic, flowing and
growing in wonderful new directions.*

Inner Beauty

I know I am a beautiful person on the inside.

I have spent much time healing my negative
images and feelings.

My inner beauty is part of my strength of
character now.

I radiate my inner beauty outward, smiling to all
I meet today.

I know some people will be able to appreciate me
and others will not, and I do not
take it personally.

What matters is that I allow myself to shine forth
with my inner radiance. My inner beauty glows
with warmth and friendship, silently uplifting all
who cross my path.

---

*I express my inner beauty as I
walk through my day.*

Assurance

I am self-assured and feel my inner strength and spiritual power.

I have the courage to move forward on my path, joyfully accepting who I am.

I meet life with the assurance that I have the skills to manage my life.

I willingly take the risks necessary to continue confronting my issues.

I have the assurance of reaching my goals.

I trust that I am fully prepared to move into my day, ready to experience all that life has to offer.

I feel the assurance that all is progressing well in my life.

Abundance

I deserve a life of abundance.

I accept my good, continually releasing all limiting beliefs of lack.

I spend quality time thinking about what I truly want so I don't clutter my world with too many things or too many experiences at once.

I have gratitude for the abundance in my life, my family and friendships, my work, my hobbies, and the service I give to making the world a better place.

I recognize my abundance in appreciating life's simple pleasures: a sunrise or sunset, the dance of light in nature, the color and scent of flowers, or the smile of a stranger.

---

*I attract abundance
in my life.*

Manifesting

I enjoy my creative power to manifest what I want for a full and abundant life.

When I determine what I want, I focus my mind on the end result and feel it strongly.

I speak clear words to myself that affirm exactly what I want to manifest.

I let go of how results manifest or when.

I pay attention to all negative thoughts that tell me I do not deserve or cannot have what I want; I then rewrite the script and use my affirmations.

I'm willing to do the work it takes to succeed in manifesting my desires.

---

*I easily manifest
what I want.*

True Success

I feel successful because my success isn't based on the images of the media or expectations of society, but on what is right, true, and of value for me.

I know that as my private goals for inner development and improvement manifest, I experience true success.

I privately celebrate the small successes in my life that others may not see or understand, such as the growth of my will, taking risks to develop one of my talents, my determination to grow, or feeling worthy of love and happiness.

I spend time contemplating, concentrating, and meditating on the meaning of true success for me.

I experience true success in my life.

Open-Hearted

I am an open-hearted person.

I open my heart to give and receive love.

I silently send positive, kind, loving thoughts to
all others and feel our oneness.

I appreciate how easy it is to learn to open my
heart with children, animals, and kind people.

I privately see all my relationships unfolding and
healing as I put more heart into them.

As I fill myself with Divine Love,
my heart opens.

Being open-hearted and aware allows me
to face difficulties that need to be resolved
and dissolved.

New patterns of wholeness emerge with the
opening of my heart center.

*I am open-hearted,
giving and receiving love.*

Letting Go

I let go of fear and insecurity and I now trust that life supports my growth.

I let go of needing family members to understand, acknowledge, or appreciate my choices as I change and grow.

I enjoy the moments when I receive their support, yet let go of unhealthy dependency.

I quietly move forward on my path and enjoy the journey.

I release everything that is not in support of my true nature and growth.

I let go of everything that holds me in bondage to what I am not.

Inner Spirit

I live with the magic of my inner spiritual life.

I allow my life to be a channel for good.

I follow my hunches and intuition
as I experience my day.

I let go moment by moment to be directed
by my Higher Power.

I follow my inner guidance as I respond to
people who are in need and set boundaries with
those who do not respect my space.

---

*I dance with the guidance and magic of
my inner spirit.*

Intellect and Intuition

I easily live in balance with my intellect and my
intuition; together they support me to make wise
choices and manage my day.

I use my concrete mind with my five senses
to see the facts.

I use my intuition and my non-tangible senses
to cut to the chase, allowing wisdom
to easily direct my life.

My intellect works in tandem with my intuition
and I appreciate both parts of me.

As I grow in awareness, I experience my intellect
and intuition acting as one.

*I allow my inner wisdom to blossom as
my intellect and intuition work in unison.*

Health

I value my health and wellness.

My body is healthy and whole and working to
the best of its abilities.

Each organ and cell works harmoniously as a
team player with all other parts of my body.

I appreciate all the physical parts and systems of
my body and the good job that each plays
in sustaining me.

I tune in to my body to find places in need.

I send love and light to any part of my system
that is hurting or not operating optimally.

I take care to get enough rest, proper food, and
activity to support a healthy body.

---

*I appreciate my
health and wellness.*

Creativity

I enjoy a creative life.

I allow creativity to flow naturally through me.

I spend quiet time in contemplation and
meditation to feel what is right to
create in my life.

I use the power of affirmation and visualization
to manifest outcomes I desire.

I remember to allow the process to unfold with
proper timing.

I creatively express my highest good when
allowing Spirit to flow through me.

I enjoy inner self-expression in my creative
hobbies and leisure activities.

---

*I enjoy inner self-expression as my
creativity flowing through me.*

Tradition

I honor the traditions of my religion,
family, and culture.

I participate to the degree that it
feels right to me.

I use rituals of my traditions to order my life,
ground me, and to fill me with the love and
connectedness of my roots.

I allow traditions to support me by anchoring
me to my past and providing security.

I choose the traditions that I want to carry
forward in my life from all presented.

---

*I honor and practice traditions
that support my life.*

Authority

I am my own authority.

I make my own decisions and take full
responsibility for them.

I respect the authority of people in power who
use power for the greater good of all.

I learn what not to do by noticing those who
misuse their power and authority.

I am in touch with my own authority and
how it affects others.

I choose to use my power wisely for
the highest good of all.

I'm aware of the higher authority I receive
from my Higher Power.

---

*I am my own authority and
use my power wisely.*

Union

I go within and quietly feel the union of all parts of myself: body, mind, and spirit.

When I am in this place of connectedness I feel the grace of being in the human experience.

This feeling of union within myself allows me to extend kindness and love easily to other people.

Feeling my union with God helps me love myself unconditionally.

Each of my important relationships work much easier when I take the time each day to center myself and feel the union and connectedness between us.

I feel joyful as I feel the union of my body, mind, and spirit with God.

Work

I have meaningful work and I find meaning
in my work.

I maximize all my talents, traits, and strengths in
the workplace, whether I'm being paid a salary,
working out of my home, or volunteering
my time.

I check my attitude periodically to make sure I'm
in the right frame of mind, as I choose to give
my work my best.

I strive for continuous improvement at work as I
do in my private life.

If unhappy I have a serious talk with myself to
determine if I need an attitude adjustment, to
communicate with someone, or find work that is
better suited to my personality.

---

*I have meaningful work and I find
meaning in my work.*

Sweetness

I focus on the sweetness of life today.

I look with curious eyes at subtle, little things happening in my day that others might miss.

I enjoy the simple pleasures in my life.

I find sweetness in sharing a smile with someone I do not know, in doing something unexpectedly from the heart for another, or in receiving a kind ear from a friend.

I find sweetness in simple pleasures, the taste and texture of my food, the sunshine streaming through my window, or watching the cloud patterns in the sky.

I brighten my day by finding the sweetness in life.

Being Right

I let go of needing to prove I'm right when a disagreement arises with another.

It separates me from others who do not share my position when I insist on being right.

Instead, I accept the fact that others may disagree with me and sometimes not care what I think or what I know about a specific topic.

As I become secure within myself, I no longer insist on being right.

I experience inner peace when I withdraw from conflict arising when I want to convince another I'm right.

I accept other points of view and let go of the need to be right.

Positive

Good things are continually happening in my life as I develop a positive mental attitude.

I see so many positive things happening in my life since I started doing the inner work necessary for my growth and expansion.

I watch my life unfold and view my experiences with a positive spin, remembering to face my issues and not deny my problems.

I release old hurts and fears and watch positive people, experiences, and results find their way onto my path.

I focus my mind on what is happening in my life that feels good and is positive.

I am optimistic and positive about myself and my future.

Death

I honor the time I have on Earth.

I release all fear of death that stops me from a
true experience of the present moment.

I understand that tomorrow isn't promised
to any of us.

I am alive right now and cherish my life.

I know there is no real death, only of
the physical form.

When it's my time, I willingly let go in order to
transition to the next level of experience.

I accept all stages of my life.

I release all fear of death and dying and
celebrate the time I have right now for
loving, learning, growing, and creating.

Transformation

I am like a butterfly just emerging from the
cocoon of transformation.

I'm different now that I have let go of
many old patterns.

Transformation is active in my life and I accept
powerful change to continue.

I grow daily into greater awareness and
acceptance of my wholeness and true nature.

Like the caterpillar changing into a butterfly,
my true Self emerges.

*I welcome the power of transformation
operating in my life.*

Middle Path

I seek to live my life on the middle path
between extremes.

I watch myself and make corrections as I manage
any tendencies to over- or under-give,
achieve, eat, etc.

I live my life to the fullest, balancing extremes in
my emotions, thinking, and actions.

I maintain inner calm as I quietly choose the
path with little drama.

The middle path allows my inner knowing
to easily surface when I need my power
and wisdom to manage issues, problems, or
challenges that arise.

---

*I consciously choose the middle path,
living my life with balance
and deep peace.*

Intuition

I am an intuitive person.

I quiet my mind periodically to listen to my wise inner voice.

I trust this inner knowing.

I allow wisdom to flow into my life, as I center myself and listen to the quiet, still voice of my inner knowing.

I have all of the protection and guidance necessary to fully accept all experiences that come my way.

I hear the silent voice of intuition whenever I ask for insight or help in making a decision or solving a problem.

---

*I trust my intuition
to protect and guide me.*

Timing

I have a good sense of timing, whether it's in communicating with another or allowing proper timing for my inner healing, growth, and expansion.

I release unrealistic time expectations.

I now know to stop pushing myself when results are not forthcoming and set a more realistic time frame for my goals.

I honor my emotional needs, as they are part of the equation of meeting my goals.

I am opening like a flower blooming in my perfect time.

I travel at a comfortable rate along my path.

---

*I have a good
sense of timing.*

Seasons

Watching the seasons in nature helps me accept
the seasons of my life.

Rather than fool myself and resist any season, I
open myself to learning the lessons
each one presents.

I explore the opportunities that each season
has to offer.

I cherish having my life and all the experiences,
both positive and negative, that have seasoned
my personality.

The joy of aging is that I no longer get caught up
in participating in the youth culture.

I accept the current season of my life.

---

*I enjoy the seasons of my life and
appreciate each new day as a gift.*

Gardener

I love being the gardener of my life.

I take great care of my garden, continuing to plant new seed thoughts of Truth.

I am vigilant in continuing to weed negative thoughts that interfere with my growth.

With loving care, I nurture the new seedlings as they grow into full stature.

My garden reflects the blossoming of Spirit within me.

I am the gardener
of my consciousness.

Results

I enjoy getting results when I set my mind
to do something.

I know the difference between reaching the goal
line and the journey it takes to meet these goals.

I remember to enjoy the process of
achieving results.

I take time to reflect upon the total experience of
striving, as well as the results.

*I enjoy
achieving results.*

Regeneration

I allow lots of quiet time when I am growing at a
fast pace so my whole being can regenerate.

As my consciousness changes, all the cells in my
body get a boost.

I continue to release old, stored emotional
baggage as I regenerate to a new level
of well-being.

I allow the old to dissolve as I renew my mind
with positive affirmations.

I experience regeneration when I take hikes in
nature, rest and sleep, daydream, and do my
spiritual practices.

*I accept regeneration
of my total being.*

Others' Choices

I understand that each person has their own path and will attract opportunities to learn and grow in awareness.

I stop when I find myself wanting to influence another's experience.

I allow others to make choices even if I would choose differently in their shoes.

I maintain my inner peace when a loved one chooses options I deem negative.

I return my focus to myself each time I get too involved with another person's choices.
I remember I'm unfinished and still growing, as well.

I offer love and support, sharing what I see only when appropriate.

I focus on my life and allow others to make their own choices.

Emotional Pain

I no longer criticize myself when I repeat a negative feeling emotional pattern.

I realize the repetition allows the intensity to grow so that my conscious mind will register an unconscious pattern.

I then can work on healing the emotional pain.

I process my emotional pain with my mind.

I journal about my issues as they come up or talk to a concerned friend or counselor.

I'm learning to make peace with the pain, breaking free from the emotional prisons I have allowed to continue within myself.

I shine the light of understanding on my emotional pain and grieve my losses.

Harmlessness

I practice harmlessness by living my life without being hurtful to myself or others in all that I think, say, or do.

I choose to live from the place of right thinking, right speech, and right action by listening to my heart balanced with my aware mind.

I spend time pondering the effects of my choices on myself and others, ahead of time, before taking action.

I live my life with awareness and practice harmlessness.

Contentment

I am content being who I am and where
my life is going.

I enjoy knowing I have the ability to actualize
many of my goals, dreams, and visions
for the future.

I find contentment in all that I have
accomplished and goals I have achieved.

I'm content knowing there are lots of exciting
things to learn about, explore, and experience
in my future.

I find peace and contentment in reading self-
help and spiritual books.

*I am content with my life
and where it's going.*

Abilities and Talents

I acknowledge my innate abilities and talents.

It's never too late to begin appreciating and using my unique gifts.

I know my talents do not have to be what traditionally is acknowledged by society.

I may write poetry, help people in need, enjoy being with children, or be in rapport with animals or plants.

I develop my special abilities and talents which fill me with joy and round out my personality.

I develop my special abilities and talents and enjoy expressing them in the world.

Family

I appreciate my whole family system and see my place as a link in an evolving system.

I look realistically at my lineage, accepting what I received, both positive and negative.

I build awareness daily of what I pass(ed) on to my children and grandchildren.

I forgive myself for not being perfect and acknowledge the positive changes I have made to improve the family system for future generations.

I continue to improve my life, which has a positive effect on all of us.

I spend time with family members I enjoy, relating openly and honestly with good communication.

---

*I love
my whole family.*

Intimacy

I learned from a teacher a simple way to explain intimacy: into me see.

I practice sharing my inner self with the people I want to get closer to emotionally.

I further build feelings of connectedness by really listening to what others have to say and making them feel safe talking to me.

As my valued relationships develop trust and acceptance, our intimacy grows.

---

*I am building intimacy in
my close relationships.*

Rules

I live by a set of rules based on my belief system.

I make a list of the spoken and unspoken rules by which I live my life.

I choose to become more aware each day of those that are hidden from me that drive me and influence my life.

I gain clarity by noticing conflicts within myself or with others.

I update the rules that I now see are negative, limiting, or even false.

I eliminate the ones that are outdated and no longer serving me and replace them with higher truths.

I am becoming conscious of the rules that guide my life and update those holding me back.

Sleep

I love to sleep after a productive day.

I allow enough time to get the rest
I need each night.

I balance sleep and rest with activity
and achieving.

I respond to my body's needs — sleeping and
resting more while in cycles of low energy and
sleeping less in times of high energy.

When I push myself for a few days because
of outer world demands and commitments, I
remember to slow it down for a few days to rest
and sleep more.

I set a routine so my body knows it's time to
let go and sleep at night, such as taking a walk,
taking a bath, journaling, or reading
before bedtime.

*I fall asleep easily and awaken
rested and refreshed.*

Efficiency

I value being efficient with my time and my activities in a day.

I use my imagination to view the most efficient way to do things, taking the least number of steps when running errands, organizing my home, or performing tasks in the workplace.

I like to save time by being efficient so that I have free time to relax and read and play.

I allow some time to be unstructured and free flowing so I do not rebel at being so overly organized.

I am efficient with my time so I have time for fun and entertainment.

Harmony

I like to live in harmony with others.

I start by developing more harmony
within myself.

I am learning to harmonize the different parts
of my personality.

I build harmony when I allow the inner child
of my past to be heard, as well as my future self
with all its wisdom.

When out of sync with another person, I take the
time to figure out what is bothering me and then
take a risk to open communication.

I am developing habits to build harmony in
my life, regular quiet time for self-inquiry,
meditation, and expressing my conflicts in a
journal or to a friend.

*I am building harmony
in my life.*

Contemplation

I like to spend some time each day
contemplating my life in order to keep
improving and learning to be all I was
created to be.

Through thinking deeply I have figured out
many things and accepted such things as: My
conditioned self is not my true Self and it gets in
the way of me knowing and feeling
my wholeness.

I shine the light of awareness into my life with
daily contemplation time.

*I take time daily
to contemplate my life.*

Satisfaction

I find a lot of personal satisfaction with my life.

I am enjoying my creative power to manifest the results I want.

I look for that feeling of satisfaction and enjoyment when spending time with loved ones, working on hobbies, or doing community service.

I am blessed with meaningful work in my day.

I find ways to increase my satisfaction with my life as I look for meaning and purpose each day.

I release situations that unduly drain, bore, or stress me and replace them with new ones with more life, creativity, and enjoyment.

---

*I feel a lot of satisfaction
in my life.*

Meditation

I live each day in a continuous meditation,
reminding myself often to stay focused
on what I'm doing.

I practice mindfulness and put my heart and
soul in all that I do, say, and think.

I take time each day to sit quietly, calming my
mind to experience deep peace and to connect to
the Source of my being.

I open to receiving guidance, motivation, and
inspiration to live my life creatively and
in service to others.

---

*I practice active meditation by focusing
clearly on what I do; I practice passive
meditation by clearing and
calming my mind.*

Thankful

I celebrate today, giving thanks for all that I have, my relationships, and who I have grown to be.

I am grateful to live a full, creative, abundant life.

I feel blessed and take the time to list all the things for which I am thankful: the specific experiences and people that have enriched my life.

I express my gratitude to several people today.

I am thankful for my life and express my gratitude.

Stillness

I calm myself with some quiet time each day to experience stillness.

In stilling my mind, I receive support and a deep connection with my higher Self.

I listen to the silent, quiet voice within which guides me and shows me the way.

I take time to feel the quiet stillness that is within me always.

I pause and take a moment to feel the stillness, especially when my day is hurried and many demands are placed upon me.

I enjoy the stillness at night or while in nature.

I notice and appreciate
stillness in my life.

Cooperation

I value cooperation with others — members of my family, co-workers, neighbors, store attendants, etc.

I know that we each will benefit from love, support, and cooperation from one another.

I see that I can make a difference in building cooperation with others.

I limit my reactions and judgments and communicate with skill and deep thoughtfulness.

I know my attitude makes a difference in building cooperation with others.

---

*I value
cooperation with others.*

Silence

Today, I observe my world and practice silence.

I listen to others and silence my reactive mind.

I live with the intention of quieting my mind chatter and receiving the guidance from my inner knowing.

I take the time to slow myself down, to practice a few moments of silence throughout my day.

I practice quieting my voice and my mind, to strengthen my ability to listen to others as well as to myself.

*I practice
moments of silence today.*

Attitude

I am in charge of my attitude.

I take notice of my attitude several times a day to see if I'm taking things too seriously and need to lighten up or am playing too much and need an attitude adjustment toward seriousness.

Sometimes I need an attitude of gratitude to quit complaining and to focus on what I like and to appreciate my life.

I monitor my attitude often in order to receive the most out of my day.

When I have a poor attitude, I take the time to ask myself what is bothering me and what I can do about it to feel better.

*I take responsibility
for my attitude.*

Partner

I appreciate my partner: a marriage or love partner, business partner, or roommate.

I focus on my partner's positive qualities and remember what attracted me in the first place.

I have unconditional love and kindness for my partner.

I see my partner's inner beauty, strength, and light.

I verbalize my appreciation.

I take obvious pleasure in what interests my partner.

Interdependent Relationships

I enjoy times of independence and times of dependence in my close relationship.

I am clear about my boundaries so that I respect my own needs while partnering with another.

I transform any relationships which have not supported me or in which I have placed his/her needs before my own.

I notice when I'm too independent and forget to receive the good things from the relationship: love, affection, caring, attention, and emotional support.

I value interdependence with the right mix of healthy dependence and independence.

I experience interdependence in my close relationships.

Remember

I remember who I am, a perfect expression of the Source.

I am an important member of the human family, unique and different from all others.

I remember my special purpose that only I can fulfill, and that is to be my Self.

I live each day with the positive intention to remember the radiant being I am that gets covered up sometimes.

I love my life when I remember who I am.

I remember who I am and feel happy being me.

Detached-Involvement

I walk the fine line between getting involved with and detaching from life situations when I become overly attached to a person, or an outcome, or try to control a situation.

I detach as others express strong emotions and go through their dramas.

I get involved to the degree a situation involves me or I believe it serves another.

I spend time thinking about the paradox of detached-involvement and practicing it.

I strive for the right balance of detachment and involvement in my life.

*I practice detached-involvement as
I experience my life.*

Beauty

I look for beauty wherever I go today.

I begin by appreciating my own beauty and
seeing myself like a piece of art.

I take the time to care about my appearance and
to express my individuality.

I see the beauty of the earth as I walk
or look outside.

I see beauty in every person I meet today.

---

*I find beauty everywhere and in
everybody, including my own.*

Equilibrium

I enjoy balance and equilibrium today.

I move forward with equilibrium as a bird does when it moves its wings in flight.

I feel steady and stable as I live my day, flowing easily with the people and events.

I stay centered by nurturing myself with kind words of encouragement, rest breaks from activities, eating reasonably, and exercising or moving my body.

Less effort is needed to move through my day when I maintain my equilibrium.

*I experience equilibrium as
I easily move through my day.*

Thank You

I have so much to be grateful for in my life.

I sit and remember all the people and situations
that have helped me become the
person I am today.

I send a thank you thought to each one.

I choose one person to call or write a thank you
letter to, expressing my appreciation for her/his
contribution to my life.

---

*I send a thank you thought to the people
who have contributed to my life.*

Addictions

I allow addictions to be a pathway to my greater
awareness and wholeness.

They teach me about blocks at the unconscious
level holding me back.

I use addictions — whether to a person,
substance, security, power, or body image — as
stepping stones to higher consciousness.

I transform my addictive behavior, not through
suppression or denial, but through receiving help
from others and from my Higher Power.

I allow a spiritual system, such as The Twelve
Steps of AA, to help me surrender my powerless
condition to my higher Self. My Higher Power
guides me past the obstacles holding me captive
to addiction, releasing me to freedom
and creativity.

---

*I use overcoming addictions
as my spiritual path.*

Ego

I love and appreciate all that my ego (little self,
conditioned self) has done to survive
and live in this world.

I am now ready to submit my ego to the
direction of my higher Self.

I am growing daily in my ability to listen to the
still, quiet voice of spiritual wisdom.

I spend quiet time daily to listen to
this higher guidance.

I joyfully relax into the process of allowing a
power greater than my little self to direct my life.

---

*I surrender my ego to the care and
direction of my higher Self.*

Senses

I honor my five senses of touch, taste, sight, hearing, and smell; they help me live in and interact with my physical world.

My senses are an important part of my inner guidance system, calling to pay attention to details in my environment.

I also honor my sixth sense of intuition and my seventh sense of spiritual oneness, helping me live in a more holistic place.

I appreciate and use all my senses to live with heightened awareness.

*I fully use and appreciate
all my senses.*

Passion

I again have a passion for living.

I focus on what things bring forth my passion — the process of self-discovery and healing to know and understand myself, developing and sharing my time and talents with others, building emotionally supportive friendships, helping people less fortunate than I am.

I am passionate about using my creativity to find solutions to my own and the world's problems.

My passion moves me forward today as I learn and grow further.

I allow my passion to move me forward today.

Cultivate

I have spent nearly a year now cultivating the
garden that is my life.

As the gardener, I have cultivated with care the
thoughts, words, and images I allow
myself to express.

I continue cultivating my garden consciously,
paying close attention to what I'm thinking,
saying, and visualizing so that I can choose
what I manifest.

I focus on the thoughts, words, and pictures that
support my healing, and release all
to the contrary.

I cultivate my mind to be here now, without
judgment, but with love, deep peace,
and acceptance.

---

*I cultivate with care what I allow to
grow in the garden of my life.*

Patience

I practice patience daily with myself and others.

I cooperate with the pace of my inner healing
and learn patience when I need to accept
the process.

I smile every time I need to slow myself down, to
let go of expectations, to be in the moment, or to
show patience with another.

I turn inward and remember to focus on the task
of the moment or a relationship's current need,
rather than only on my interests and goals.

I take deep breaths whenever I lose patience,
to slow my pace and regain balance.

*I practice patience with myself and others
as my day unfolds.*

Friendship

I value my circle of friends.

I connect emotionally with my close friends.

I am available for them and they are there for me, sharing our inner journey with each other.

Close friendship is part of my foundation, supporting me as I weather the storms of life and celebrating with me when I have a breakthrough or accomplish a goal.

I exchange love and support with my friends.

I open my door to new friendships.

I am blessed with
good friendships.

Mastery

I am the master of my own life and future.

I grow daily in understanding how to overcome negativity still influencing me.

I take full responsibility for changing what I do not like and creating what I do want.

It's no longer a crisis if I make a mistake or a "wrong" choice as they are part of how I am learning to master my life.

I take risks daily to gain further mastery over my destiny.

As I grow more aware each day, I appreciate all that I have mastered in my life.

I listen to the authority of my spiritual Self as I continue mastering my life.

***I am gaining mastery
over my own destiny.***

Free to Be

I am free to be me, my spiritually evolving Self.

I am free to creatively express and grow into my
potential, all I was created to be.

I allow my spiritual essence to shine
and it feels great.

I continue going within to clarify and redefine
my wishes, hopes, dreams, goals, values, and
beliefs to create in alignment with
my true needs.

My freedom grows daily as I allow my true Self
to direct my life.

*I am free
to be me.*

New Results

I continue improving my life and set
new results in motion.

I think about and study why I do certain things
that do not support my growth.

I choose one aspect about myself that I would
like to change.

I use my new awareness to find hidden
agendas, competing needs, guiding beliefs, and
suppressed feelings.

As I discover what motivates this behavior,
I plan how I will do things differently and
achieve new results.

I set, as a high priority, healthy ways
to meet my real needs.

---

*I am setting new results
in motion.*

Emotional Boundaries

I choose clear emotional boundaries with others,
especially with people with whom I'm in
a close relationship.

I check with myself first when another
wants me to do something.

I listen to myself so I can clearly say "yes" or "no"
to support my best interest.

I remember to love myself during the times it
takes courage to say "no."

I am strong now and can easily risk rejection
when another person isn't pleased
with my answer.

I have strong emotional boundaries now.

---

*I set clear emotional boundaries and
have the right to say "no" as well as
"yes" to others.*

Good

I know that I am good.

My intentions are to be my best at each moment.

I separate my unwanted habits and behaviors
from who I really am.

I forgive being hard on myself and
for not being perfect.

I am growing daily in living my spiritual path
and being my true Self.

I feel my innate worth and wholeness.

---

*I know
I am good.*

Smile

I smile to myself when I have a
happy feeling inside.

As my good feelings grow, it automatically
shows on my face.

I willingly express to others the good feelings
I'm feeling on the inside.

When another smiles at me, I feel uplifted and
get a boost of positive energy.

Sharing a smile unites us for a moment.

Genuine smiles open doors with others.

*I give others
a smile today.*

Leader

I am developing the qualities of good leadership.

I am responsible, affirming, a good
communicator, and a good observer
of circumstances.

I have self-discipline, the ability to listen, am
interested in others, and I can lead by example.

I do my inner work daily to continue growing
and healing, as I can only lead as far as
I have traveled.

I like to lead interested and curious others to the
path of self-discovery and inner healing.

*I am
a leader.*

Truth

I have been learning the truth about many things in the past year, both personal truth and universal Truth.

I now know the truth about who I am and what I deserve.

I am a loving, powerful, growing, aware person.

I deserve a life to pursue my dreams, to self-actualize my potential, to discover personal happiness, and to be creative.

My new level of self-esteem allows me to accept these good things and more.

I feel my spiritual wholeness and a connection to the greater plan and purpose for my life.

I am a spiritual being, waking up to my true nature and magnificence.

I know the truth
and it sets me free.

Harvest

I am experiencing an abundant harvest of
goodness in my life.

I have grown light years in accepting myself and
taking responsibility for my own life.

I am proud of myself for all the diligent inner
work accomplished and for the self-discipline
I have mastered.

I am enjoying new outcomes from all the seed
thoughts planted and cultivated in the garden of
my consciousness this past year.

I am grateful for deepening the spiritual power
guiding my life.

*I am enjoying a bountiful harvest
of goodness.*

Winter Solstice

I go with the flow of the new season.

I feel the rhythm of winter slowing me down to contemplate at the end of a year-long growing season.

I feel a sense of completion after this cycle of change and growth.

I slow down to allow the roots of my consciousness to grow to greater depth.

I have spent a year cultivating my garden, getting to know and love myself, and building a stronger spiritual foundation.

It's now time to rest and quietly assimilate what has been gained. I allow the winter solstice to remind me to go within to enjoy a time of deep peace and celebration.

I slow down and go with the rhythm of the winter solstice.

Simplicity

I appreciate simplicity.

I am ready to make changes to simplify my life.

I sit and think about the things that drain my energy and keep me from enjoying the simple pleasures in life.

I prefer to use my time doing the things that support my growth and are fun, like spending time with people who I really care about.

Simplicity means I will have to be clear with myself about what I need to release — from activities and relationships to clearing clutter.

I let go of people and situations that complicate my life.

**I create simplicity
in my life.**

Joy

I allow joy to light my way today.

I feel the joy of the holiday season and enjoy
seeing people more open and loving.

I open my heart and joyfully feel my connection
with all people.

I am centered and fulfilled now and every day.

I am joyful to feel one with myself
and all creation.

I feel the light of day shining brightly as I
continue to awaken, as the darkness of being
unconscious is behind me.

---

*I spread my radiant joy
and light to others.*

Rebirth

I prepare for a rebirth as I leave behind a year
of inner work and transformation that totally
changed my life.

I open my consciousness for more expansion.

I spend the day in an active meditation,
continually tuning in to my deeper rhythms.

Wherever I go, I notice the spiritual
essence of all Life.

I feel the joy and fullness of the season.

I attune myself and warmly connect, if even with
just a smile, with each person I meet today.

*I accept rebirth as a continuous
opportunity for new beginnings.*

Higher Consciousness

The seeds of spiritual awareness have given birth to new levels of consciousness within me.

I use the Christmas story, no matter my religious preference, to remind me of its deeper meaning.

I allow the story to inspire me to accept the symbolic birth of Christ Consciousness (Cosmic Consciousness, Self Realization) into my life as I strive to live this Truth.

I accept the deeper meaning of the birth of the Christ Child to deepen my spiritual connection to all Life.

I accept Higher Consciousness in my life.

Retreat

I rest and nurture myself today.

I treat myself kindly.

I retreat to spend time reviewing my year.

I notice where I have mastered many lessons, improved my self-esteem, and grown into a better person.

I make an honest assessment of all my issues, behaviors, thoughts, and feelings that still need attention.

I write my insights in my journal.

I take quiet time to retreat today, reviewing my year and making preparations for beginning anew in the coming year.

Seeker

I am a seeker after greater wisdom and truth.

I seek greater understanding of myself and the great experience of Life.

I wish to go further on my journey to understand more about the mysteries of life, creation, birth, death, levels of consciousness.

I seek to know God on a personal level more and more each day.

I find answers by talking to people wiser than myself. I study Universal Truth in the teachings of world religions, being mindful to stay away from dogma or any teachings that teach superiority or separation.

I connect to Universal Truth in contemplation and meditation.

I am a seeker
of Universal Truth.

Appreciation

I appreciate exactly where I am right now on the path of my life.

I release judgments of past behaviors, unrealistic expectations, and choices that slowed me down or took me on side trips.

I forgive myself for all unwise choices.

I acknowledge myself for all the growth and expansion achieved.

I appreciate the perspective I now have on life.

I appreciate all I have learned from each of my experiences, as I weave them together into the tapestry of my life journey.

*I deeply
appreciate myself.*

Letter

The future calls me forward, full of potential.

I take steps today to activate the most wonderful, enlivening future I can imagine.

I write a letter of intention to myself today that I will read in one year.

I list things I want to experience, learn, and accomplish in the next year.

I add personality traits I wish to modify or transform.

I clarify what is practical to achieve in one year.

I write a letter of intention to myself today.

*Purification**

I prepare myself to go to a new level of success in
practicing the awareness I have gained
in the past year.

I trust Spirit to continue guiding me in new
directions for my highest learning
and development.

I purify myself with proper diet, thought, speech,
and spiritual practices.

I am a clear channel for Love to flow
through me to serve others.

*At noon Greenwich time (7:00 AM Eastern Standard
Time) on December 31, I align myself with people all
over the world by reading the World Healing Meditation
(begins on page after the December 31 passage). I can
also choose my own prayer or meditation.

---

*I purify myself to be a clear channel of
love and light.*

World Healing Meditation

I am part of the critical mass necessary to move humanity into peace and harmony.

I join my consciousness today with all others creating world peace.

I understand the power that my prayers and meditations have as I join like-minded others of all faiths, religions, and views.

I visualize all people of the world empowered by love, free-will choice, and connection to their spiritual power.

I participate in the mind-link by reading the World Healing Meditation on the next page or another one of my choosing.

I am one with all minds that join for world healing and peace.

World Healing Meditation

By John Randolph Price

In the beginning.
In the beginning God.
In the beginning God created the
    heaven and the earth.

And God said Let there be light;
    and there was light.

Now is the time of the new beginning.

I am a co-creator with God, and it
    is a new Heaven that comes, as
    the Good Will of God is
    expressed on Earth through me.

It is the Kingdom of Light, Love,
    Peace and Understanding.

I begin with me.

I am a living Soul and the Spirit of
    God dwells in me, as me.

I and the Father are one, and all
    that the Father has is mine.

In Truth, I am the Christ of God.

What is true of me is true of
	everyone, for God is all and all is God.

I see only the Spirit of God in
	every Soul,

And to every man, woman and
	child on Earth I say: I love you,
	for you are me.

You are my Holy Self.

I now open my heart, and let the
	pure essence of Unconditional
	Love pour out.

I see it as a Golden Light radiating
	from the center of my being, and
	I feel its Divine Vibration in and
	through me, above and below me.

I am one with the Light.
I am filled with the Light.
I am illumined by the Light.
I am the Light of the world.

With purpose of mind, I send forth the Light.

I let the radiance go before me
	to join the other Lights.

I know this is happening all over
the world at this moment.

I see the merging Lights.
There is now one Light.
We are the Light of the world.

The one Light of Love, Peace and
Understanding is moving.

It flows across the face of the earth,
touching and illuminating every soul
in the shadow of the illusion.

And where there was darkness,
there is now the Light of Reality.

And the Radiance grows,
permeating, saturating every form of life.

There is only the vibration of one
Perfect Life now.

All the kingdoms of the earth
respond, and the Planet is alive
with Light and Love.

There is total Oneness and in this
oneness we speak the Word.

Let the sense of separation be dissolved.

Let mankind be returned to Godkind.

Let peace come forth in
every mind.

Let Love flow forth from
every heart.

Let forgiveness reign in
every soul.

Let understanding be the
common bond.

And now from the Light of the
world, the One Presence and
Power of the Universe responds.

The Activity of God is healing and
harmonizing Planet Earth.

Omnipotence is made manifest.

I am seeing the salvation of the
planet before my very eyes,
as all false beliefs and error
patterns are dissolved.

The sense of separation is no more;
     the healing has taken place,
     and the world is restored
     to sanity.

This is the beginning of Peace on
     Earth and Good Will toward all,
     as Love flows forth from every
     heart, forgiveness reigns in
     every soul, and all hearts and
     minds are one in perfect
     understanding.

It is done. And it is so.

Index

Subject	Date
Abilities and Talents	November 13
Abundance	October 15
Acceptance	September 6
Achieving	January 11
Active Intelligence	June 28
Addictions	December 5
Adventure	August 21
Aging	March 20
Allowing	October 6
Anger	August 23
Animals	August 6
Appreciation	December 28
Approval	February 23
Asking	April 21
Assignment	August 14
Assimilating	February 21
Assurance	October 14
Attitude	November 27
Authority	October 25
Authority of My Soul	May 13
Autumn Equinox	September 21
Avoidance	February 25
Awareness	January 13
Balance	April 26

Beauty ....December 2
Being Genuine ....May 10
Being Open .... April 24
Being Right ....October 29
Birthday......................... September 7
Blame .... January 25
Body Awareness .... May 2
Body Metaphors ....June 16
Boundaries .... January 30
Catalyst .... September 10
Cause and Effect.....................June 18
Challenges............................ April 6
Children............................ July 27
Choices........................... January 8
Clearing ....June 12
Co-Creating..................... September 17
Color ....August 12
Comfort...........................June 29
Communication .... April 16
Communion ....June 15
Comparison........................January 12
Compassion.......................August 5
Conditioning........................... June 1
Confidence .... March 17
Conflicts........................... June 23
Connectedness ....August 7
Consequences .... April 17
Contemplation ....November 20

Contentment.....................November 12
Contribution.........................May 16
Control............................August 29
Cooperation ....November 25
Courage .... March 16
Cultivate........................December 9
Creativity........................October 23
Critical Mass......................August 27
Criticism .... September 3
Curiosity .... May 14
Current Perspective .... July 25
Daily Goals .... May 8
Daily Purpose ....October 4
Death ....October 31
Deep Peace ....August 11
Deepening Relationships............August 17
Dependency ....June 24
Deserving .... March 22
Detached-Involvement ....December 1
Dislikes.............................June 30
Double Agent .... September 22
Efficiency........................November 18
Ego ....December 6
Emotional Boundaries.............December 15
Emotional Pain...................November 10
Emotional Reactions .... January 16
Emotional Strength .... May 7
Emotional Victim................... January 20

Encouragement. . . . . April 30
Enjoyment . . . . March 30
Enlightenment . . . . .August 24
Enmeshment. . . . . April 25
Enthusiasm . . . . .October 5
Equilibrium . . . . .December 3
Evaluating Myself. . . . . May 3
Everyone Is My Teacher. . . . . March 3
Evolving. . . . . April 9
Excitement. . . . . April 23
Exercise . . . . September 5
Expectations . . . . .February 26
Family . . . . .November 14
Family History . . . . .June 27
Fear. . . . . .February 20
Feeling Blue. . . . . July 19
Feeling Good. . . . . January 9
Feelings . . . . January 19
Focus . . . . May 6
Food. . . . . .August 3
Forgiving Myself. . . . . January 22
Free To Be .December 13
Freedom. . . . . July 7
Free-Will Choice . . . . January 14
Friends. . . . . September 9
Friendship . . . . .December 11
Garden . . . . September 1
Gardener . . . . .November 6

Gentle Strength. . . . . May 24
Giving. . . . . February 3
Goals . . . . January 28
Good . . . . .December 16
Good Intentions . . . . April 29
Goodness. . . . . April 3
Gratitude . . . . .February 27
Greater Meaning. . . . . September 16
Grief. . . . . July 21
Grounding. . . . . March 1
Growth. . . . . April 2
Happiness . . . . March 28
Harmlessness .November 11
Harmony . . . . .November 19
Harvest. . . . . .December 20
Health . . . . .October 22
Healthy People . . . . March 14
Heart . . . . .August 1
Helping Others . . . . May 11
Higher Consciousness . . . . .December 25
Honoring Myself. . . . . May 1
Humility. . . . . May 26
Humor . . . . June 9
I Am . . . . July 26
Important . . . . September 11
Improvement. . . . . September 20
Improving a Relationship . . . . February 5
Information. . . . . March 12

Inner Balance . . . . .August 10
Inner Beauty . . . . .October 13
Inner Child . . . . .October 10
Inner Female. . . . . March 7
Inner Freedom . . . . May 25
Inner Guidance. . . . . September 13
Inner Knowing . . . . January 10
Inner Male. . . . . March 8
Inner Peace . . . . .February 19
Inner Resistance . . . . April 22
Inner Spirit . . . . .October 20
Inner Strength. March 23
Inner Vision . . . . April 8
Inner Work . . . . June 25
Integrating. September 14
Integration. . . . . June 4
Integrity. . . . . January 24
Intellect and Intuition . . . . .October 21
Intellectualizing . . . . .February 17
Interdependent Relationships. . . . . . .November 29
Intimacy. . . . . .November 15
Intuition. . . . . .November 3
Journal Writing. March 9
Joy. . . . . .December 23
Joyful . . . . June 22
Judgmental . . . . May 27
Knowing Self. . . . . April 14
Leader . . . . .December 18

Learning. . . . . July 17
Letter . . . . .December 29
Letting Go . . . . .October 19
Life as a Process . . . . September 24
Life-Style Changes . . . . June 6
Light. . . . . July 5
Limitations . . . . July 14
Living Love . . . . July 28
Looking Within . . . . .August 18
Love . . . . May 12
Loving Kindness. . . . . March 27
Loving Myself. . . . . .August 26
Loving Relationships . . . . July 10
Love Versus Like. . . . . .February 16
Magical Day . . . . .February 29
Maintenance . . . . September 2
Making a Difference. . . . . May 9
Manifesting . . . . .October 16
Masks. . . . . March 25
Mastery . . . . .December 12
Meaning. . . . . March 15
Meditation. . . . . .November 22
Memorial Day. . . . . May 30
Middle Path. . . . . .November 2
Mirrors. . . . . .February 6
Mistakes. . . . . January 18
Money . . . . September 29
Mother/Father/Mentor . . . . May 29

Motivation...................................May 18
My Body ....April 7
My Father ....August 31
My Life.....................................April 11
My Mother...............................January 31
My Rights................................August 25
My Shadow ....May 20
Naive ....September 30
Nature ....March 19
Needs and Wants ....September 25
Negative Thoughts ....July 9
New Beginning.......................January 1
New Ideas ....June 2
New Life.................................August 4
New Results.......................December 14
Nourishment...............................June 3
Now ....September 28
Nurturing..............................January 6
Nurturing Others ....August 13
Offensive Behavior....................October 11
One Day at a Time ....March 5
Open-Hearted.........................October 18
Opening Communication...............June 10
Open-Minded..............................May 15
Openness....................................March 6
Opportunities ....March 29
Organic ....October 12
Organization................................June 5

Others' Choices. .November 9
Partner . . . . .November 28
Passion . . . . .December 8
Past Suffering . . . . January 15
Pathways . . . . September 19
Patience . . . . .December 10
Patterns . . . . April 18
Pause . . . . September 12
People. . . . . September 23
Perceptions . . . . .August 20
Perfect Order. . . . . April 5
Perfection. . . . . April 12
Perseverance . . . . April 13
Physical Appearance . . . . .August 2
Physical Health . . . . May 28
Plants . . . . .August 8
Playfulness. . . . . April 1
Playing My Hand .June 19
Polarities . . . . .October 1
Poor Me . . . . April 15
Positive. . . . . .October 30
Positive Intention . . . . September 15
Potential. . . . . January 2
Power . . . . July 12
Power to Choose. May 4
Preferences . . . . January 27
Problems . . . . .February 13
Process. . . . . March 18

Projection . . . . March 2
Prosperity . . . . February 1
Protection . . . . May 5
Proud . . . . July 16
Purification . . . . December 30
Purpose . . . . February 10
Quality of Life . . . . September 18
Questioning . . . . February 15
Real Needs . . . . May 19
Reawakening . . . . August 15
Rebirth . . . . December 24
Receiving . . . . February 2
Recovery . . . . July 29
Regeneration . . . . November 8
Relating with Feeling . . . . August 19
Relationship . . . . June 11
Relaxation . . . . March 24
Releasing Pain . . . . January 26
Religious Guilt . . . . June 26
Remember . . . . November 30
Remembering . . . . July 24
Repressed Feelings . . . . April 19
Resistance . . . . June 7
Resolving Issues . . . . April 20
Responsibility . . . . January 7
Restructuring . . . . October 9
Results . . . . November 7
Retreat . . . . December 26

Right Action .... April 27
Risks.............................. March 10
Roadblocks .... July 3
Roles.............................. July 18
Rules..............................November 16
Sacred Space ....February 11
Satisfaction ....November 21
School of Life ....February 12
Seasons...........................November 5
Secret .... July 8
Seeker............................December 27
Self-Acceptance .... July 30
Self-Appreciation .... January 4
Self-Assurance ....June 13
Self-Care .... April 4
Self-Esteem .... April 10
Self-Improvement...................February 4
Self-Inquiry........................ May 23
Self-Talk.........................February 24
Senses...........................December 7
Service .... September 26
Shame..............................May 17
Silence ....November 26
Simplicity.........................December 22
Sleep.............................November 17
Slowing the Pace..................... March 4
Smile.............................December 17
Soul.............................. July 6

Spontaneity . . . . .August 22
Spring Equinox. . . . . March 21
Spiritual Essence . . . . .February 8
Spiritual Guidance . . . . .June 8
Spiritual Heritage .October 7
Spiritual Nourishment. . . . . .February 9
Spiritual Power . . . . .August 30
Spiritual Practice . . . . September 4
Staying Present . . . . July 11
Stillness . . . . .November 24
Strengths . . . . .June 20
Stress. . . . . .October 3
Subconscious Mind . . . . July 20
Success . . . . July 15
Summer Solstice. . . . . June 21
Sunlight . . . . .August 9
Survival . . . . May 31
Sweetness. . . . . .October 28
Synchronicity . . . . July 1
Talents . . . . .February 7
Teachers. . . . . July 31
Tension. . . . . .October 2
Thank You . . . . .December 4
Thankful. . . . . .November 23
The Earth. . . . . July 2
The Journey. . . . . March 31
The Land of Opportunity . . . . July 4
The Path. . . . . July 22

Thoughts . . . . January 29
Time . . . . July 23
Time Alone . . . . March 13
Timing . . . . .November 4
Tolerance . . . . July 13
Tradition . . . . .October 24
Traits . . . . September 8
Transformation . . . . .November 1
Transitions . . . . .October 8
True Power . . . . March 26
True Success .October 17
Trust . . . . June 14
Truth . . . . .December 19
Unconditional Love . . . . January 5
Union . . . . .October 26
Unwanted Behavior . . . . January 21
Valentine . . . . .February 14
Value . . . . .February 22
Value-Judging . . . . January 17
Vessel . . . . .August 16
Visualization . . . . March 11
Vulnerability . . . . January 23
Weeding the Garden . . . . June 17
Weighing Consequences . . . . May 22
Well-Being . . . . May 21
Well-Nourished . . . . February 28
Wellness . . . . .February 18
Wholeness . . . . .August 28

Winter Solstice .December 21
Wise Use of Power . . . . April 28
Work. . . . . .October 27
World Healing Meditation . . . . .December 31
Worthiness . . . . January 3
Wounds . . . . September 27

Self-Help Books By Suzanne E. Harrill

Books For Adults

Seed Thoughts for Loving Yourself
Cultivating the Garden of Your Mind Day by Day
ISBN 9-781-883648-16-9

Enlightening Cinderella
Beyond the Prince Charming Fantasy
ISBN 1-899171-58-4
E-book edition.
ISBN 1-883648-18-1

A Simple Self-Esteem Guide
Booklet, saddle stitch binding.
ISBN 1-883648-09-2

Empowering You to Love Yourself
E-book edition only. ISBN 1-883648-10-6

Inner Fitness for Creating a Better You: Six Lessons for
Building Greater Awareness, High Self-Esteem, Good
Relationships, and Spiritual Meaning
Spiral bound. Worksheets to copy for
educational purposes.
ISBN 1-883648-11-4
E-book edition.
ISBN 1-883648-12-2

Books For Adolescents

Empowering Teens To Build Self-Esteem
ISBN 978-1-883648-04-6

EXPLORING * CONNECTING * EMERGING:
Adolescent Self-Esteem
Curriculum. A guide for parents, teachers.
Ages 11 – 17. Co-authored with Charlye Jo Ivy.
Spiral bound + worksheets to copy.
ISBN 1-883648-05-X

Books For Children

I Am a STAR, My Building High Self-Esteem Book
5 X 4. Rainbow colored pages. Ages 2 – 9.
ISBN 978-0-9625996-3-7

I Am a STAR Self-Esteem Cards
40 affirmations on rainbow pages + star eraser,
zip baggie. Ages 2 – Adult.
ISBN 1-883648-08-4

Order online at www.InnerworksPublishing.com
Sign up for free online, self-help newsletter
to spark the inner journey.